James 4:8

DRAWING NEAR

JARED MONTANA

A Mere Fisherman

Table of Contents

Foreword

"Loving You Back" by Luke Bower

You've always loved me
Though you're nowhere near my mind
But still you want me
You call my wicked soul your prize

But when I look into a mirror I see something unloveable
But when I look at you all these mirrors start to crack

I think I'm loving you back
I think I'm starting to see
How Good you are to me
I feel you pulling me in
I hear you whispering truth
You say "nothing in this world could ever love you like I do"
I think I'm loving you back

You always knew me
Even when I knew you not
You look right through me
Past my smile faked facade

But when I look into a mirror I see something unlovable
But when I look at you all these mirrors start to crack

I think I'm loving you back
I think I'm starting to see
How Good you are to me
I feel you pulling me close
I hear you whispering truth
You say nothing in this world could ever love me like you do

Oh God of creation there's not a thing I've
Done that could render me worthy of your love
But you wrote the story and signed it with
Blood and the flames meant for me drowned
In grace like a flood

I think I'm loving you back
I think I'm starting to see
How Good you are to me
I feel you pulling me close
I hear you whispering truth
You say nothing in this world could ever love me like you do

Chapter 1

Faiths' Equipment

I have always been a fisherman- my dad taught me. When I was just a few years old, my parents took my two siblings and me on vacation during the Summer. We stayed in an old, musty, one-story condo. The condo was vaulted in case of flooding because hurricanes and flooding were relatively prevalent, so parking was under the apartment. Once opening the front door, you were inside the living room. Hanging on the walls were paintings of sunsets and sunrises, a school of wooden fish, and water stains on the ceiling. There wasn't much to the living room other than a TV and an old, fold-out couch where my two older siblings and I would sleep. Ten feet in front of you was the kitchen, and if you looked at your ten o'clock, you could see the hallway to the only bedroom. It was probably one of those couches where if you slapped it, a dust cloud would fly up, but we didn't care. We were just happy to be there. I was just happy to be there.

My dad liked to fish, so he had brought a couple of fishing poles and left them outside below the porch. Right behind the condo, there was a dark-green lagoon with a dock. I always loved that dock because you could see fish jumping out of the water. My brother and I used to swim in the lagoon while my dad fished, and we'd see them

1

jumping and say, "Look! It's a flying fish!". Then, one morning, I woke up naturally at sunrise and decided to go fishing. Keep in mind I was only a few years old. I was capable of making decisions, but I couldn't think through them. What if there was no bait? What if I fell in the water without my floaties? What if I caught a catfish, and it barbed me? Heck, what if I caught a fish? I wasn't capable of thinking through "what if's." I was simply reacting on instinct.

I got out of bed without waking up my siblings and went outside. By all means, I was unequipped, but I knew I wanted to catch a fish. Once I was outside, I could smell the morning beach lagoon breeze. Without putting shoes on, I walked down the old, splintery stairs in hopes of finding a fishing pole. I got lucky- there was a leftover, dried-up worm on a hook. Now, I'm not a gambling man, but I don't think it was a coincidence. God knew that someday I would be telling you this story. So I grabbed the rod and walked down the dock all by myself. I didn't know what I was doing. Previously, my dad had always baited my hooks, set the hook in the fish's mouth, and unhooked the fish. I was unequipped with the proper knowledge.

As I approached the end of the dock, I got eager. My heart started to pound with excitement; my mind started racing with everything I could catch. I remember letting my little toddler toes dangle off the side of the dock and trying to cast my line as far as I could. In reality, my dried-up worm didn't make it far, but in my inexperienced toddler mind, it would do just fine. I didn't have a bobber. No, I simply had a line, a hook, and a dried-up worm. If you aren't familiar with this setup, you don't watch the bobber go underwater. Instead, you are watching your line in hopes of seeing it start moving away from you- almost as if it is running. So here I am, unequipped with extensive knowledge but equipped with only the necessary knowledge. I dropped my bait into the water. After a few seconds, I see my line start to run. I realized that I forgot to set the hook, but I did remember to reel. The next thing I knew, I had a little fish on the hook flopping on the deck. Now what?

I hadn't thought this far ahead, so I relied on the only knowledge I did have: "Daddy can do it!" I picked up my rod with the fish still attached and ran back into the condo. Once I got inside, I saw my dad standing over the stove cooking breakfast. I happily shouted, "Daddy! Look what I got!" and as he turned, I saw three facial expressions go from one to the other- happy, worried, and confused. First, he was delighted that I was happy about catching a fish. But, he was worried because his wife would find out that he let their youngest child go unsupervised, near a body of water, for an undetermined amount of time. Then he became confused because he didn't know how I did it. So he told me, "Good Job!" as he unhooked the fish and said, "Now go throw it back in the water and quickly come back!"

I've always been a fisherman; even when I didn't think I was. Just because you don't know who you are in God's eyes or what you are to be for God's kingdom does not mean that you are not already it. God already knows how he intends to use you for His kingdom. In his mind, you are who you will become already. At this point, the only thing missing is that you aren't adequately equipped... or are you?

Looking back, I realize that I wasn't "adequately equipped." I had no rod; I had no bait; I didn't know how to unhook a fish; I had no logical reason to think I could catch a fish. The only thing I had was desire, a calling if you will. I was unequipped until I accepted my calling. Now let me clarify; I'm not saying that all desire is a God-given calling, but I think that sometimes a God-given calling can be driven by passion. By our standards, I was unequipped. But by God's standard, I was equipped. He knew what I needed and when I needed it, and he put them in my path in His timing- not mine. He just wanted me to follow that calling. So I walked by faith- I followed that calling. 2 Corinthians 5:7 says to "walk by faith, and not by sight." Sometimes our "sight" is found in reason- hindsight, foresight, etc. We use our knowledge to determine our actions. But our sight, or knowledge, is misleading. Illusions fool us all of the time. That is why we are called to walk by faith, not sight. When we walk by faith, we walk by God's knowledge, and God is all-knowing. Remember in the story where I realized that "Daddy can do it?" At what point in our adult lives does it become apparent that God can do it? He can handle our burdens, our weight, and our stress. He gives rest to the weary (Matthew 11:28). As adults, we rely too often on our sight. We need to have a factory reset to that of a child so that we can walk by faith. Matthew 18:3 says, "*...unless you turn and become like children, you will never enter the kingdom of heaven.*"

With that being said, children are never equipped. That's why they have parents to guide them. They have much to learn. Likewise, we have a father to guide us. When it comes to doing God's will, God calls us all. He wants us to walk in faith, not by sight- To act on the calling regardless of not knowing if you even have bait, regardless of not knowing what to do with the fish. I am a fisherman. I simply catch "fish". I have been called to be a fisher of men. But I am not alone in this calling; you are called too. God equips us with His Word- The Bible. This book you are reading is not meant to replace the Bible by any means. No, this book will teach you how to apply His Word to your calling.

Chapter 2

Mere Fisherman

I am a Mere Fisherman. When I was 20 years old, I remember feeling like nothing I did truly mattered. It seemed like nobody cared about what I did or what I said. I was going through so much mental pain that I was blinded to the truth. I had just moved 200 miles away to a city where I knew nobody. It was an old town that thrived on death and decay.

One night, I felt so insignificant that I went to Waffle House by myself. I was never a drinker, so this was my version of going to the bar. I remember walking towards the bar stools and taking my seat, looking at where my future All-Star meal would be plopped in front of me, not taking the time to speak to anybody. I quickly ordered a cherry vanilla Coke and drank it while my thoughts ran wildly. I couldn't seem to escape my thoughts. They chased me like an endless wind on a cold, weary night. I was lost. Alone. Insignificant. Soon after that, I found myself 80 miles from my new "home." For some reason, I had convinced myself that it was a bright idea to go for a drive, not knowing where my destination would be. Perhaps I drank too much cherry vanilla Coke. I didn't know what it was at the time, but something about the stillness during that drive healed me. It was God's voice.

In the still drive, I realized my faith had been wavering. Now, what is wavering faith? When your faith is wavering, in short, you will begin to follow the desires of your sinful nature. Examples of this include sexual immorality, impurity, lustful pleasures, idolatry (placing priorities over God), sorcery (yes, this includes the rising "power in crystals" movement), hostility, quarreling, jealousy, outbursts of anger, selfish ambition, dissension, division, envy, drunkenness, and wild parties (Galatians 5:19-21). What does it look like to have wavering faith? Here is what my life looked like while my faith was wavering: self-dependency, control issues, excessive planning, self reasoning without considering scripture, having priorities outside of God, and a lack of praying. If you see this in yourself, you should work on your faith. If you see this in others, you should show them mercy to calm them while hating the sin that contaminates their lives (Jude 23). My faith was undoubtedly wavering. Matthew 17:20 says that the "faith the size of a mustard seed can move mountains," so, at this point, my faith must've been the size of a Helium atom. Over the next few months, God would speak to me in ways he never had before. In this, he taught me about the disciples and so much more.

Four of the Disciples, Peter, Andrew, James, and John, were all Fishermen (Matthew 4:18-22) and possibly Thomas and Nathanael (John 21:1-3). Another disciple, named Matthew, was a tax collector (Matthew 9:9). Then, if you are familiar with Judas, you will know that he was a thief (John 12:6). In the eyes of the world, the disciples of Jesus Christ were incapable and unqualified of such a calling. In the eyes of the world, they were nobodies. In the eyes of the world, *they* were Mere Fishermen... I don't think you get it. What qualifies us to do God's will? The very fact that **WE ARE UNQUALIFIED**.

I am writing this to you today because I, myself, am unqualified. Not because I have been adequately trained (I haven't) but because I have been called, just as you have. I once heard this phrase that went something like, "God doesn't call the equipped; he equips the called." By now, you might have recognized the phrase, "Mere Fisherman." This book is for the newly saved and the recurrent, backsliding Christian. It is not for the faint of heart nor the prideful. It is for those who walk humbly in Spirit. This book is not meant to replace the word of God but is instead a tool purposed to aid in understanding. You will be tested in times of praise (Proverbs 27:21), so remain in giving all glory to God because when the time of praise ends, the world will look down on you for your faith and will mock you for your actions. In the world's eyes, we are "Mere Fishermen," but to God, we are so much more. We are Loved. He sees who we are and what we have done and will do, yet He chooses to love us perfectly. He casts out our fear and wipes away our every tear. Some disciples were fishermen by trade, but *all* were Fishers of Men by call (Matthew 4:19). We are all disciples. We are all Mere Fishermen.

Chapter 3

Fishers of Men

It was a hot, mid-summer afternoon in Georgia. The birds were chirping. The squirrels were hopping on the ground as they frantically looked for food hidden under the leaves. In the distance, you could hear two young boys laughing with insurmountable joy. It was funny! Their laughter sparked joy within you; it was contagious! First, you would listen to a "Woooaaahhhhh!" and then an ominous muffled crashing sound, as if there were a wave or splash. Then things would go quiet. A few seconds would pass, and then you'd hear that unmistakable laughter. Then a handful of minutes later, the process would repeat itself.

I was one of those boys. I was seven years old, and my early childhood best friend and I were out of school for the summer. It was a Sunday afternoon; we had just left Sunday school, where we learned about the disciples and how Jesus called them to be fishers of men (Matthew 4:19). Like every other boy our age, we each had a bike, but we didn't use them as every other boy did. My buddy had figured out that if you rode the bikes down the hill without wrecking, you would get an adrenaline rush. At the bottom of this giant hill was a pond. I'm not sure if it was by accident or on purpose, but my buddy quickly found out that the water would serve a dual purpose of both breaking his fall and cooling him off. When he came up out of the water, he shouted, "You've gotta try this!" So, like Dom Toretto riding to save his family, I, too, blazed down this hill in hopes of experiencing the excitement that I read on his face.

When I crashed, God protected me because I found a rather sharp stick surrounded by many other sticks, yet I had no scratch on me. So my friend and I started cleaning out our crashing area of miscellaneous debris that could cause us harm. I don't recall how many sticks we moved, but I will never forget the chant we shouted. From the shallows walking towards the deep and vice versa, we cried, "I'm a fisher of men! I'm a fisher of men! I'm a fisher of men!". No matter the size of the stick and no matter the depth of the water, even if we couldn't stand, nothing could stop us from singing our chant.

The world is a lot like that pond. As innocent children, we weren't aware of the dangers held within, nor are you and I aware of the dangers that constantly surround us that God protects us from. There is no telling how many hooks were hidden by the muddy cloud of water, how many Alligator Snapping Turtles we stepped next to, how many snakes we almost grabbed hiding under the sticks, or what kind of bacteria or parasite we could've picked up from that stagnant cesspool of water. But God protected us. We had the time of our lives thriving on His protection. Two seven-year-old boys knew that they were called to be fishers of men and were unashamed to shout it; even if it was their last words before sinking underwater.

Can you imagine if we, as adults, had this same mindset? If we had that same level of faith? If we had that same level of determination to accomplish God's will? The results would be exponentially more outstanding than they are now. Why? Because people run from their calling. People are scared to share the gospel. People are hesitant to "go and make disciples of all nations" (Matthew 28:19). That is what being a "fisher of men" is. Yet we are hesitant to be who we are called to be. God's will is going to be carried out regardless of if you think you can outrun it. God uses both the good and bad things in this world to accomplish his will. No matter how hard you try or how fast you run, God's will is going to prevail because he already knows what you are going to do and has made his will in accordance with all actions.

Can you imagine how infinitely more efficient we would be if we had the faith of a child? We wouldn't care about the dangers of this world- Fear of rejection, persecution, judgment, or temptation. If we had proper faith, these are all things that would go ignored because our God is bigger than them. Our God is bigger than our fear in and of itself. God himself says to fear not because he will strengthen us, help us, and uphold us (Isaiah 41:10). If we believe His Word to be accurate, who are we to doubt the Almighty God? He is the Alpha and the Omega, the first and the last (Revelation 22:13). God will have the final say over all of our fears. He has given us no reason to doubt him, but rather every reason to trust him. Yet, when we lean on our understanding, our sight, like we ought not to do (Proverbs 3:5), it causes us to have doubts. So why do we doubt?

We certainly don't doubt because he first doubted us. No. We love because he first loved us (1 John 4:19). We learned how to doubt from somewhere, something, or someone but not from God. God has shown us love, grace, and mercy. So if our doubt isn't rooted in

God, where did it come from? In simple terms, you learned it from the experiences around you. From the time you first opened your eyes, you saw doubt in the people around you. But if we time travel to the fall of man (Genesis 3), we know that doubt is first introduced by Satan, the snake, to Eve. We see it in verse 1 when Satan says, "Did God *really* say....". I honestly think that doubt is the silent killer of faith. It is what started the fall of man. When we doubt ourselves and our abilities, we doubt God's perfect plan for our lives. God gave us our gifts and talents for a reason, for a purpose. A purpose that is not to go unnoticed but instead achieved. Why is it so dangerous to doubt? Because when we doubt ourselves, we doubt God's plan. When we doubt God's plan, we lose sight of our calling to be fishers of men. Doubt is the slow, thoughtful rot of faith. Some people allow their faith to be overtaken by doubt, by decay. Do *not* be this person. Don't get me wrong; skepticism is reasonable. True skepticism of the Bible affirms the validity of it, but doubting yourself leads to doubting God which leads to destruction.

When we rely on ourselves for strength, we will not find it. We won't be able to pick ourselves back up. However, when we rely on God, he can pick us up from our rotting corpses and renew our strength (Isaiah 40:31). We are imperfect people living in an imperfect world; through belief in Jesus Christ, we have been cleansed of our impurities (Romans 3:23, 1 John 1:7). We are all fishers of Men. Yet, all of this means nothing if we don't have faith- if we don't trust in God. How can we trust in something that we don't even know what it is? What, or who is God?

Chapter 4

Who is God

Shortly after my wandering 80-mile escapade (Chapter 2), I realized that I didn't know God. I grew up in church and heard about God my whole life- I could even tell you all about how the Bible describes God, but I didn't KNOW him. It's like one of those situations where you know OF somebody- you hear about them all the time, but you don't know them personally. That's how my relationship with God was. Sadly, this is where it gets confusing. I had believed in Christ, but I didn't know God. I wholeheartedly believed that Jesus died and was resurrected so that I could be cleansed of all my sin, but I still didn't know The Father. I had the head knowledge- enough to teach the youth at church, but I didn't have the heart knowledge. Thankfully, God revealed my lack of heart knowledge during my midnight adventure. I would soon begin the long, extensive journey to finding this "heart knowledge." I believed in God, but I didn't have true faith in God. I knew I needed to find God. I knew I needed to know him.

Because I was the youth leader at my fathers' church, I had to be at church on Wednesdays. I had a hectic schedule at the time- I was an overtime college student, worked 48-60 hours a week on an ambulance, and was behind the steering wheel about 30 hours every week just commuting between my responsibilities. As a result, I didn't sleep much. Even when I had the chance to sleep, I struggled because my mind continuously held the weight of depression. They say that you experience peaks and valleys in life, but this was a hole at the bottom of a desert valley. A hole that I had dug myself. Since then, I've found the idea of somebody digging their own grave relatable. There's no telling how many times I contemplated driving my car off the road into a ditch.

To this day, I'll still say I've never thought about committing suicide. That's because I never actually wanted to die, I wanted something else. I thought I knew what that something was, but I never got what I thought I wanted. I didn't want death, but I contemplated dangerous actions because of my mental state. I felt so insignificant. It didn't matter what compliments anybody told me about myself at this point in my life. Compliments couldn't get past the thick cloud of self-judgment that loomed around my head like that of a sandstorm in a desert. How did I escape the sandstorm? I was able to find something far more valuable than what I thought I wanted. It was nothing that I did. Not directly, that is. It would take me a while to learn that God had better plans for me than to doubt his creation and His perfect will. Yet, here I am today, healed. God knew what I needed, and it was Him.

Wednesdays weren't days off, but they were the only days that felt like a day off. Wednesdays were special. I would get up, work out, then drive to the church. I'd get to the church around noon, so I had 6 or 7 hours to myself before the youth would start arriving for service. I always felt peace there. I'd drive my car as close to the pond as I could, pop the trunk and grab the Life Application Study Bible that my parents had bought me as a graduation gift then grab a notepad. Once I had these necessities, I'd sit at the picnic table by the water. There's no telling how many days I sat under that large Oak, but they all seem to have the same setting in my memories.

When I reminisce, every Wednesday was always a beautiful day. There was a slight breeze with the smell of nature hitchhiking through the wind. As I looked around to take in God's beautiful creation, I'd see purring doves, schools of minnows, a lone blue crane, and a beautiful sky. Sometimes the wind made it hard to read my Bible because the pages would start flipping without consent, but I didn't care. Soaking in the truth of God's word and his presence was plentiful for me. I'll never forget my first time drawing near to God while sitting on that picnic table. I didn't know what I needed to read in The Bible; I just knew I needed to read it. So, like every other Christian in times of desperation, I flipped to a random page, and that's where James 4:8 stuck out to me. It read, "Draw near to God, and He will draw near to you...." It was then that I realized I didn't know God. How could I draw close to something if I didn't even know what it was? So that's where I began on my redemptive, fulfilling journey. These hours of alone time with God were the only things that I honestly looked forward to every week. These hours of alone time with God were what brought me out of my self-dug valley.

Fun fact, I always have an internal dialogue in my head. I remember asking myself, "What is Love?" No, really. What is it? Is it a feeling? Sex? A choice? My dictionary says it is "an intense feeling or deep affection for," but that doesn't sit right with me. Since God

17

is the author of Peace (1 Corinthians 14:33), I believe that Satan, the adversary, is the opposite, ergo, the author of confusion. If Christianity is about God extending His love to us, then it would make sense for Satan to distort what love is. This could explain why love being a "feeling" didn't sit right with me. Thankfully, The Bible tells us what love is in two different locations. We no longer have to ask ourselves "what is love" because God is Love (1 John 4:8). Now that we know that God is love, we can cross-reference scripture and learn the characteristics of God. 1 Corinthians 13:4-8 says, "Love[God] is patient and kind. Love[God] is not envyous, boastful, proud, or rude. It[God] does not demand its way. It[God] is not irritable, and it[God] keeps no record of being wronged. It[God] does not rejoice about injustice but rejoices whenever the truth wins out. Love[God] never gives up, [God] never loses faith, [God] is always hopeful, and [God] endures through every circumstance... [Love/God] lasts forever." Then it clicked. Satan has distorted the definition of Love so that the unsaved can't comprehend how a "nonphysical being" can love them. Satan deceived the world into believing that Love is only a physical thing, e.g., feelings/sex, so we can't comprehend the nonphysical aspect of Love that God offers us- Himself. Allow me to clarify that God's Love, Himself, can manifest itself in many ways, including physical. The effects of His love can present themselves physically. Still, the free gift of Love that He extends to us is no longer physical but rather a spiritual gift. A spiritual gift that Satan will do anything to ensure you don't accept.

Love is not a feeling, nor is it sex. Love, on our end, is a choice that we have to make daily, but to God- Love is Him. He is the very essence of Love. Love is not a choice He has to make because He is Love. My words cannot begin to describe the feeling you feel once you truly know God and experience His love. This feeling is so rare amongst "Christians" because some aren't truly saved. They have the head knowledge but never the heart knowledge. This would explain how some "Christians" walk away from the faith- they were never truly saved and never truly experienced His love, so they were never truly a part of the faith (1 John 2:19). If you haven't felt His love to the degree that I'm describing, don't worry. It took me a couple of years after this journey that I'm showing you for me to recognize this feeling. This was the beginning of a faithful journey to discover who God is. I had always heard Christians talk about "God's Voice," but I didn't quite understand it. I had never heard an audible voice speaking to me, so the idea seemed too bizarre and abstract, so I knew this was something I had to explore. What is God's voice, and what does it sound like?

Chapter 5

God's Voice

Over the next seven days, I listened to an Audiobook titled "Experiencing God" by Henry Blackaby while driving between responsibilities. I often structured my long, 4 hour morning commutes by blasting hype music as loud as possible to wake me up. After 30 minutes of screeching until I lost my voice, I'd change the music to an early 2000's Christian worship music playlist. I would open my mind during the worship and soak in the words. Usually, after 30 minutes or so, I would turn the radio completely off. This is when my mind would wander like the Israelites-often becoming lost. This was when I became vulnerable.

The sandstorm of self-judgment would reinstate itself, and I'd doubt myself. I'd doubt God. I'd ask God "why?" and then plead with him for the things that I thought I wanted. It wouldn't take long for me to become emotional. I could only focus on my mistakes and regrets. When I finally crawled out of that exhausting abyss, I began to lean on my understanding. I started to plan strategies to dig out of the grave that I had dug for myself. But I was only digging deeper. Once I recognized the dark state that my mind had become, I'd turn on the Audiobook for 30 minutes. There's no telling how long I'd allow myself to drive without the radio on. It was different every time, but usually, I had just enough time to cycle through everything only one time. All I know is that those 4-hour drives went by really fast. Sadly, I don't remember most of what Henry Blackaby said. Still, I will never forget these words: "God speaks to us in four ways- Prayer, The Bible, Church, and Circumstance." Little did I know that his insight would shape the way I studied God's word from then on out.

A few days later, I was sitting in the same comforting spot as I was just a week before. However, this time was a little different because now I had a study plan. I wanted to study God's voice. I wanted to have perfect clarity. A few days prior, my mom showed me a studying technique that I was eager to check out because it personalized God's word. She called it the "Letter to God" format. If you read chapter 1 to this book, then you know this book you're reading is a tool meant to help you apply God's word into your calling. With that being said, what I'm about to show you can help you find your individual calling as well as help you understand and apply the words of The Bible into your life. I'm going to walk you through this study method so hang tight because it'll change your life like it did mine. This letter that I write will be from my perspective, sitting under that large Oak at that point in my life.

If you're able, grab some paper and a pen. After this brief explanation, I will depict how it should be formatted. At the top of the page, write the date, name, and topic. We are going to find God's Voice together. On your first line, write "Dear God," and I want you to write a prayer to God about the topic you are studying- what you want to learn, where you're struggling, etc. Be as detailed as possible. Some Bibles have a concordance in the back of the book- find the word/topic you want to study, and it'll show you biblical references about that topic. The reference ought to have a brief description next to it, read those and write down on your paper the corresponding verses that match the descriptions that most stick out to you. Then, write "Dear *insert your name here*," and begin reading the verses that stuck out to you in another paragraph. If you don't have a concordance in your Bible, Biblegateway.com and openbible.info have search bars- search your topic. This is where it is necessary to write down (in your own words) what the Bible reference says but write it on your paper so that it's as if God is speaking to you. You can do this with as many or few verses as you'd like. I'd recommend starting with three verses per God's biblical response, but if there are more verses on the topic then space out the verses to be three per God's response, at least. After you've done this, read God's letter to you and then start the process over. Then, write another prayer responding to God's response. Repeat this process as many times as necessary. If this doesn't make sense, that's okay. I'll show you what I mean. Sometimes in your written letters, a recurring theme or topic will stand out and come to mind- keep the study going. Do the same process but with the new topic. Let's write a "letter to God" together on the topic of "God's Voice."

Date: N/A   Topic: God's Voice   Name: Jared Montana
"Dear God, You are absolutely glorious. Holy is your name. Glory be to your wonderful name. I pray that you enable me to become a vessel for your kingdom, that you use me to carry out your will in a positive manner so that I can impact this world for your kingdom. God, sometimes it's hard to hear your voice,

and I'm stuck. I don't know what decisions to make because I don't know your will since I don't know your voice. God, I pray that you show me how to hear your voice and know your will for my life. I know I'll make mistakes in this life, but I know that if I put my trust in you, you will help me and won't mislead me."

"Dear Jared, my sheep know my voice. They use this to guide them, and they follow it (John 10:27). If you love me, you will keep my commandments (John 14:15). If you struggle to hear my voice, it is because you don't know me (John 8:47). If you have The Holy Spirit, it will teach you everything you need to know about my will and will help you remember the word (John 14:26)."

"Dear God, Are you saying that if I don't know your voice, then I am not saved? I don't know why I'm asking for clarification. Your word clearly says it. If I understand correctly and am saved, your voice will guide me, and I will follow it. So am I saved? God, I don't hear your voice. I don't know your voice. Show me who you are so that I can hear your voice. Descend on me the Holy Spirit; I want to know you. I want to be saved. I want to carry out your good and perfect will."

"Dear Jared, I'm standing at the door. I've been knocking for a while now. All you have to do is open the door, and I will come in (Revelation 3:20). If you want to find me then look for me with all you've got. If you do, you will find me. If you ask, you shall receive (Matthew 7:7-8). Reach out to me through prayer, and I will show you things you didn't know before (Jeremiah 33:3). When you pray, I want you to seclude yourself. Go to a closet or room where you can close the door. When you pray, pray to Me, The Father, in secret (Matthew 6:6). I want you to be still and secluded because I speak in a whisper (1 Kings 19:12). When you hear my voice, it ought to be what guides you like a lit path in the middle of the dark (Psalm 119:105)."

"Dear God, it's open! Come into my house and make yourself comfy! Make this house your own. I'm sorry for the delay. I heard the knocks, but I didn't think it was you. How can I continue to look for you? Where can I find you? Where can I start looking? I'm asking that I find you, your voice, and ultimately your will. You say that if I seek, I shall find God, so I'm seeking you. Show me you. You're right about the prayer thing, you have already begun to show me so much, and I will continue to block out all distractions so that I can solely focus on you. Thank you, God. I promise to follow your guidelines as best I can. God, the clearer you reveal yourself to me, the harder it'll be to deny that you're there at the door knocking. Make it obvious. Give me a sign when I need it."

"Dear Jared, The Bible is all that you need. All of the answers you are looking for are contained within. You are holding my written word. My breath created your Bible. You can find my voice there. I want you to use it for teaching, correcting both yourself and others, verifying, and training. I want you to train people into equipped Godly men and women (2 Timothy 3:16-17). That is my will for you. I have revealed myself to people in many ways. You should know that I am real because the things I have created are real. No man is without excuse (Romans 1:19-20). You will find me through scripture. You may ask me to confirm guidance through circumstance(Judges 6:36-40) but do not test Me, the Lord your God (Matthew 4:7)."

"Dear God, Thank you. I just read through our letter, and you didn't fail me. You showed me how to hear your voice, find your words, and your will for my life. Your Love is abounding and never fails!"

It's as simple as that. We completed that Bible study together, and it wasn't planned ahead of time. That was a raw, genuine study. Typically, because I noticed a theme of God's will, I would continue studying that topic. Then that topic would lead to a study on wisdom, then fear, then love, and so on. I encourage you to stop reading and write a Letter to God on those topics right now. This method helps illuminate God's Word if you do this study right. It is not a new revelation because it all comes straight from The Bible. There is always more to learn in The Bible. If you want to know God's voice, then put yourself in a position where you can hear his voice. You wouldn't go to Miami, Florida, if you were trying to find the Rocky Mountains. Put yourself where you want to be, in God's presence, in a secluded room with no distractions. Allow him the opportunity to speak to you through one of the four avenues of communication.

Prayer should be the most prevalent form of communication, the Bible second, church third, and then circumstance.

Before we start asking for signs, I recommend that we do a word study on it. Learn the appropriate times to ask. There is a fine line between asking for confirmation in circumstance and testing God, a line you don't want to cross. What do Henry Blackaby and I mean when we say God can speak through the church? We aren't saying that the church walls grow lips. No. The body of Christ, all righteously saved individuals, are the church (Hebrews 10:25). You should seek advice from the church after you have prayed about something and searched for God's answer in The Bible. I think it is wise to ask people knowledgeable of The Bible so ask your mentor or pastor. So what does all of this mean? When something arises in life, here's what you do: pray to God first, look for answers to your questions in the Bible second, run to the church if you're unable to find biblical answers, and then ask God for guidance through circumstance if needed.

If you want God to speak to you, you must first become saved. God knows all things, but he hears the prayers of the one who carries out his will (John 9:31). What is his will? It is to glorify him in all that we do in broad terms. To be slightly more specific, read 1 Thessalonians 5:11-24. If we want to know God's voice, we need to be still and listen. Some Christians claim to hear God speak to them audibly. I have never heard God speak to me in an audible voice. I haven't been blessed with that gift, but when we have his word and the answers we need, why would God need to speak audibly? I once heard a pastor say, "if you want to hear God speak audibly, then read The Bible out loud." In John 10:27, Jesus says, "My sheep hear my voice, and I know them, and they follow me." So we ought to know God's voice and follow his directions. When we read the Bible, we can learn many promises. One of which is that "God will never leave you nor forsake you" (Deuteronomy 31:8). So do not fear because perfect love casts out all fear, and God will always keep his promises.

Chapter 6

God's Promises

I've always been amazed by perspective. When I was a toddler, my world was brighter. I remember running through the house screaming joyous laughter while my brother would chase me around. After running by my mom, I'd run to my sister's room for protection. She was the oldest of us, and she had authority over my brother. From my brother's perspective, he wasn't feeling good, so he was chasing his younger brother out of his room so that he could lay back down. He'd run by our mom, nipping at my heels, and hounded me until his annoying brat of a little brother ran into his sister's room, slamming the door closed. From my sister's perspective, she would be peacefully writing in her diary in the privacy of her room. Then, out of nowhere, she'd hear frantic screaming and get distracted, but only for a second. Then, like an explosion, her door would burst open just to be slammed as if it was the aftershock. From my mother's perspective, her oldest son's medical bills were adding up. She would see her boys running around the house, putting on a joyful fake smile for the youngest, then showing a compassionate, loving stare at the oldest. Then, as she heard a door slam, it'd remind her of the heavy hospital door closing.

My brother was sick. He had Crohn's disease (which hid the celiac disease that went undiscovered for another 15 years) and was in and out of the hospital for weeks at a time. Crohn's disease is a chronic inflammation of the intestines, often associated with ulcers. It doesn't sound serious on paper, but it can be life-threatening. As a toddler, I couldn't grasp the idea of my brother being that sick. I'll never forget when my mother asked me to make sure he was still breathing. She was sitting on an out-of-fashion flower-decorated pillow in this white rocking chair with a Bible in her hands. It was the same rocking chair she used to rock me to sleep with. As I walked over to her, I could see the worry on her face, yet she instilled peace in me. My brother had been sleeping for three days. Everything he ate caused him to be in immeasurable pain. She said, "Jared, watch my stomach while I breathe. Do you see how it moves? You may have to watch for a while, but whenever I take a breath, It'll move out. After a short pause, she asked, "Can you do something for mommy? Go to bubby's room and watch his stomach for a moment, then come back and let me know if it moves out." From my perspective, my brother hadn't played with me for a few days, and I thought he was mad at me. I was hesitant, but I went anyway.

Once I got to his room, I started watching his stomach. His stomach was moving. I must've been loud because my brother woke up and turned towards me. I saw this as an opportunity. "Scotty, let's go play!" To which he sluggishly said, "okay." I ran back to mom's room with such excitement that I got a carpet burn on my foot when I stopped. I told her that his stomach had moved, and he said he wanted to play. Her face lit up with joy. When we went back into his room, there he was, sleeping in a ball, with pain written all over his face.

I've always been amazed by perspective. I was too young to understand anybody else's perspective, but I was able to see that they had their own. As I got older, I learned more about my mom's perspective. I had always seen her reading her Bible, striving her best to make every aspect of her life about carrying out the words of The Word. Growing up, I didn't know what fueled her desire to follow God's word, but now I do. She knew what life was like without God, and she wanted nothing to do with the absence of God.

When she was 30, her repressed memories had returned. Mom wasn't raised in a good, christian household. Instead, she was verbally, mentally, and sexually abused- taken advantage of and ignored. In the eyes of her parents, she was worthless and a disgrace. When these memories resurfaced, she knew she couldn't rely on the family, but she had to rely on something. She had been going to church for a while, but it wasn't until her memories resurfaced that she made God her strong foundation, her all and all, her refuge (Psalm 91:1-16). God promised her safety just as he has promised you- those who live in the shelter of the Most High.

Have you ever wondered what the promises of God are? There are hundreds! But most of them start with surrender. After all, there is no greater love than to lay down one's life (John 15:13) which is precisely what Jesus did for you. Since Jesus died for you, it is the least you can do to live for Him. If you genuinely love God, you will sacrifice your life for his glory. Before you get mad at me, no, it is not God's will for you to die right now. We can sacrifice our life by giving up our wants, possessions, desires, and daily comforts. What I'm trying to say is that "the greatest among you must be servants" (Matthew 23:11). We must become Servants for our Lord.

Like I said before, by the time my mom was 30, she had been going to church for a while. One day, while studying Matthew 14, she prayed, "God, you can have me. I surrender. Use me." Her story began with surrender. At that moment, she "saw a flash" of her childhood. Her repressed memories flooded in. Another promise God has made is that "whatever is said in the dark will be brought to light" (Luke 12:3). Allow me to clarify, this is about judgment day, but God chose to reveal these memories(things done in the dark) to her. I think her story is best told in her words:

"After these memories were revealed, I thought I was losing my mind, so I sought help. I became depressed and wanted to end it all, but then I realized how much God loves me and that he has a plan for my life and that my past does not define me and that God has a purpose for the pain- it wasn't all for nothing. God was with me that day, but he has upheld me since I was conceived and has carried me since birth. He sustained me and rescued me. He repressed those memories until the time was right to protect me. His words became a lamp unto my feet and a light unto my path (Psalm 119:105). He saved me then, and he continues to save me now. God is unchanging in his Love. Ever since that realization, Christ has been my rock. My firm foundation. I believe in every promise in His Word for my life and the life of my children. Isaiah 46:4 says, *'I will be your God throughout your lifetime- until your hair is white with age. I made you, and I will care for you. I will carry you along and save you.'*

I've always been amazed by perspective. It's easy to get swallowed by the worries of this world and only see things through our eyes. Don't do that! It is dangerous to only look at the world God created through our perspective because our limited worldview is restrictive to God's love. To understand the promises that God has given, you have to first begin to understand things from His perspective as best you can. Understand that he wants you to love him. Everything He does is for Love. If you want to reap the rewards of God's promises, you must first surrender just like you would in any loving relationship. A good marriage is when both spouses choose to love each other, dying to self daily, sacrificing their wants for their spouse's benefit. Our relationship with God ought to be the same! He has already sacrificed Himself for you, now you ought to sacrifice your fleshly desires for Him! There are countless promises found throughout scripture, so I urge you to write a "letter to God" on the topic of His promises. In the meantime, there are a few things that you need to know. First, God always fulfills his promises at the right time, which are in his time (Exodus 2:23-25). Second, have faith in his timing (Genesis 16:1-3, Genesis 21:7). Third, have confidence in God because of all that he has promised you (Joshua 14:6-12). God's promises ought to keep you content (Phillipians 4:10-14). God will guide you, guard you, and protect you. God has written you a letter. But for most people, it is sitting on their nightstand collecting dust. The only way to know His promises for you is if you open up your Bible, the letter, and read it. Surrendering is essential to God, and it takes having faith on our end- faith that He is who He says He is, faith that He will fulfill all of His promises, and faith in salvation.

Psalm 91(NLT)- When in doubt, call 911 (Psalms 91:1)

"Those who live in the shelter of the Most High will find rest in the shadow of the Almighty. This I declare about the Lord: He alone is my refuge, my place of safety; he is my God, and I trust him. For he will rescue you from every trap and protect you from deadly disease. He will cover you with his feathers. He will shelter you with his wings. His faithful promises are your armor and protection. So do not be afraid of the terrors of the night, nor the arrow that flies in the day. Do not dread the disease that stalks in darkness, nor the disaster that strikes at midday. Though a thousand fall at your side, though ten thousand are dying around you, these evils will not touch you. Just open your eyes, and see how the wicked are punished. If you make the Lord your refuge, no evil will conquer you if you make the Most High your shelter; no plague will come near your home, for he will order his angels to protect you wherever you go. They will hold you up with their hands so you won't even hurt your foot on a stone. You will trample upon lions and cobras; you will crush fierce lions and serpents under your feet! So the Lord says, "I will rescue those who love me. I will protect those who trust in my name. I will answer when they call on me; I will be with them in trouble. I will rescue and honor them. I will reward them with long life and give them my salvation."

I'm not affiliated with these websites, nor do I know all they support. Still, if you want more quick information on God's promises, you can visit these two websites:

https://www.gotquestions.org/great-and-precious-promises.html
https://www.compassionuk.org/blogs/gods-promises/."

Chapter 7

"Godcidence"

I've always been a fan of the outdoors. When I was a senior in Highschool, my friend group often went camping. Sometime around September, we started planning a road trip around the U.S., stopping at National parks. I didn't care for most of the parks; the one I cared most about was Glacier National Park in Montana. As you can tell from the front cover, I may have a bias. I've always wanted to go to Montana because it's my name! So, in preparation for this trip, we all decided to go camping one October weekend.

It had been a good day! We all got out of school and went our separate ways to gather supplies. My best friend, who wasn't a part of this friend group, called me and asked if I wanted to go fishing. I couldn't refuse. I went home, loaded up the truck and attached the boat, and we went to the lake. I planned to go fishing for a few hours, then come back and go camping- meeting my friends right after eating dinner around 8 p.m. The fishing was decent, and we caught a couple. On the way home, I was stressed because I would be a bit later than expected. Suddenly, there were brake lights as far as the eye could see. We were stuck in traffic. What was usually a 1-hour drive turned into a two-and-a-half-hour drive. I texted my friends and let them know that I would be late by the time I met them at the campsite.

By the time I got home, I was tired. A day of school, on the water, and traffic had drained me. I texted a buddy in the camping group, and he said they would text me whenever they got back from dinner. A couple of hours go by, and I get no text, so I wind up falling asleep. The next thing I know, it's morning. I had missed my opportunity to go camping. I look at my phone, and the text reads, "We got in a bad wreck. The car fishtailed, flipped, and rolled multiple times, falling off into a 20-foot ditch. Somebody got ejected, another broke his hip in numerous places, another broke his femur, but everybody else seems to be miraculously okay." I was shocked. By nothing short of a Miracle, not a single person died that day. God's angels, commanded by God's will, protected those men that day. These men had promises from God that were not going to be broken. It wasn't until later I realized that had I been there, statistically speaking, I would have died. For that kind of trauma to happen without any deaths is statistically improbable in and of itself- now add one more body to the equation. I can't speak for the rest of those men, but here's what I can say- That one event, though not directly affecting me, reconfirmed God's existence.

In Matthew 11:20-22, Jesus denounced the people who had seen his miracles and still chose not to believe. How often are we like those people? The evidence of God is all around us! We see His miracles portrayed through modern medicine when a woman chooses to love a man (because I know that doesn't come naturally- Men are stupid) and through his creation. Romans 1:19-20 states that *"no man is without excuse"* because they can see his creation and "invisible qualities-

eternal power and divine nature." Woe to the men and women who refuse to acknowledge the apparent miracle of life!

Time and time again, God has reconfirmed his existence to me because I constantly find myself in doubt. Doubt is the slow, thoughtful rot of faith. Before I began to devote my life to The Lord seriously, I doubted often. I didn't see or feel the effects of sin. Because I felt no consequence to my actions, maybe this "God" in the sky didn't exist. I doubted Him. Usually, when these doubts plagued my mind, I'd begin to sin more- almost as if I was testing God to see if He was there. Then, it was when I needed it most that he'd reveal himself to me. He would remind me that He never left my side.

God has revealed himself to me many times. Before you accuse me of being a heretic, know that I'm not claiming to have seen God's face. No, I've seen the effects of God. When you see ripples in a lake, do you see what caused the ripples in the water? Do we question where it came from or what caused the ripples? We don't see the rock that caused it, but we do see the ripple. For those who aren't blinded by their sin, they know that a rock was the cause of the ripple. However, those whose sin blinds them cannot see the rock, which is why they come up with different possibilities. "Maybe bird poop fell from above!" But those whose sin has been dealt with and cleansed would say, "No, it can't be that. We would see residual effects and discoloration of the water's surface if that were the case. It was a rock." The blind sinners might say, "Maybe a bird picked up a rock and dropped it in the water!" But a seeing sinner would say, "why would a bird be carrying a rock? That makes no logical sense." A seeing sinner would say, "Clearly, somebody threw a rock into the water."

God has revealed himself to me many times. A few months after I was born, I was diagnosed with a rare skin disease and asthma. The doctors didn't want to test my allergies at that age, so instead, they gave my mom a list of allergies most children with that disease had. This list included shrimp, hot baths, cheese, ant bites, bee stings, alcohol, trees, grass, and about 70 other things. As you can imagine, my childhood memories are plagued with carrying around that Ziploc "medicine bag"- the most critical medication being my Epi-Pen. Because of my allergies, I wasn't expected to lead an everyday life.

Shortly after the infant diagnosis, while standing in an office, a gun misfired and shot a bullet within an inch of my head. I would've been hit if my mom had been resting on her other hip. A nearby stranger heard the commotion and saw the result; He looked at my mom and said, "God's hand is on that boy!" But you know, maybe that is just a coincidence.

As I got older, I began to lead an everyday life. I quit carrying my Medicine bag. When I was 12, I went for a lung production test. The doctors wanted to monitor how much air I could draw in, hold, breathe out. They would often test this by giving me computer generated birthday candles to blow out. I could never blow all the candles out. My lungs weren't up to par. This test wasn't new, I had done it every six months of my life, but this time was different. The results showed me having an average lung capacity. A miracle had taken place. Also, by this time, it had become apparent that I wasn't allergic to many of the items on my allergy list because I loved cheese and hot baths. I could go by each line item, but the results are the same; most of my supposed allergies were no more. I say "most" because I fear some of the items to this day, so I refuse to test them out. I don't eat shrimp because the nurse told my mom that I needed to eat in front of the ER doors if I ever decided to eat shrimp. I'm still working on conquering those fears, but it helps to know that if I live in the shelter of the Most High, he is my refuge and safety (Psalms 91:1). But you know, maybe that miracle is just a coincidence.

When I was twelve, we had a little rabbit "farm." It was my job to ensure they had water. Usually, I'd grab a bucket and walk to the pond 50 feet away, then fill it with water. This time was different. We were in the middle of a drought, so the pond's water level had decreased significantly, and I couldn't get water from the pond. So because of the drought, I now had to walk 150 feet to the house and fill the bucket from the water spigot. One day, as I was approaching the house, I heard a loud crash. I looked back and saw that a giant limb, easily weighing a couple of hundred pounds, fell right where I would've been standing had I been filling up the bucket from the pond. "Thank God for the drought" became my text signature for the next month or so. But you know, maybe that was just a coincidence.

When I was twelve, our church had a water tubing Men's retreat to the mountains. To go tubing, one had to be at least 13 years old, so that I couldn't go. I was bummed. I remember begging my parents, saying, "please let me go! I know I can't go tubing, but I can still sit in the cabin! I don't want to be left at home alone with the girls!" No matter how hard I pressed, my parents still wouldn't let me go. In the cabin, the beds were upstairs, and the kitchen was downstairs, which was on the second story. Before leaving to go tubing one day, the men decided to try and smoke a brisket on the charcoal grill while they were gone, which was on the second story deck. Sometime after they left, a bear smelled the brisket, climbed up the pole supporting the kitchen deck, and knocked over the grill to get the brisket. In doing so, the coals were hot enough to catch the wooden deck on fire. According to the fire department, the cabin had practically burned to the ground before they even got the call from a neighbor. At the time, I had a bad habit of playing games on my iPod with headphones in. I know that I wouldn't have been aware of my surroundings if I had been there. I would've been trapped on the 3rd story on the side of the mountain with fire forcing an unplayable hand. By the time I saw the fire, it would've been too late. I was delivered from that situation by not being in it. But you know, maybe that is just a coincidence.

One April weekend, at the end of my junior year in Highschool, I wasn't feeling well. On Saturday, my brother played collegiate baseball just a few hours away from home. The night before, my mom asked me if I'd go with her the next day. Again, I wasn't feeling well, but I didn't want her to go alone, so I told her to ask me again in the morning. Early the following day, she woke me up and asked, "how are you feeling? Do you feel up to going?" I didn't, but I felt guilty, so I told her I felt well enough to go. It was a two-day baseball series, so my brother let my mom and I stay at his house. The following night, at 3 in the morning, my dad calls and says, "don't worry. I'm fine, the dogs are fine, but the house is on fire." We tried our best to sleep after that phone call. Twelve hours later, as soon as the game finished, we headed to what was left of home.

Dad was there, salvaging some of what he could. The entire house didn't burn down this time, but we would later find that smoke ruined everything. The fire chief had said that the fire started in the kitchen. My dad made french fries the night before, and when he finished, he left the grease in the pan to cool off and slid the pan to a cold eye on the stove. We would later find out that particular stove had a recall because some models turned on randomly. So it was a grease fire. The fire chief said that all the smoke from the kitchen went straight into my room because of how the vent system was. He added that I would've died in my sleep had I been there. But I wasn't there. Something made me feel guilty and compassionate for my mom for possibly driving by herself. But you know, maybe it was a coincidence.

These stories can go on for days. The point is this- How many instances of "coincidence" have to occur for it to no longer be a coincidence. How many different rock ripples does it take to realize that somebody is throwing rocks into the water? How many different "coincidences" does it take for somebody to realize that we are not here by chance? Humans are in the perfect environment on a self-sustaining perfect earth, which is the perfect distance from the sun, which is in the perfect location in the galaxy. Humans are the perfect embodiment of a creator. We are not made by chance. The brain telling the heart to beat while the heart supplies blood to the brain to tell the heart to beat does not occur randomly. Without one, the other does not exist. There is an element of faith for belief in God's word,

I'll admit. But using the mind God gave, you can extrapolate that it doesn't take much faith to believe there is a creator. It takes more faith to believe there is no creator than it does to believe there is a creator. Everything in the natural world has a creator. A duck has a mommy duck and a daddy duck. A painting has a painter. A seed has a tree that it fell from. You have an intelligent designer that created you. Like I said before, there is always an element of faith when it comes down to it. So what is faith? What is saving faith? How do we obtain it?

Chapter 8

Saving Faith and Repentance

Jesus, while on earth, lived a sinless life. Jesus was the perfect, unblemished lamb. When he died on the cross, he became the perfect sacrificial lamb that would be the ultimate sacrifice. His sacrifice ended our bondage and enabled us to be free from the consequence of our sin. Jesus bore the punishment of our sin on that wretched, splintery cross. Believing in his death and resurrection is the basis of our faith and salvation.

Allow me to start by saying salvation and faith are different. Many Christians use the terms interchangeably. It is not wrong, but to have a proper understanding, we must first build a firm foundation. Let's start by defining faith. Faith, simply put, is a belief that results in action. Faith is also the "assurance of all things hoped for. It is the evidence of things we cannot see" (Hebrews 11:1). God's grace saves us through faith (Ephesians 2:8). There is nothing we can do to deserve God's grace. Our faith is not a "works-based" salvation. We are imperfect people living in an imperfect world. In Matthew 19, Jesus tells the parable of the Rich young man. The man wanted to know what he could DO to get into heaven- what works he could do to earn a spot in heaven. Ultimately Jesus would say in verse 26, "Humanly speaking, it is impossible. But with God, everything is possible." There is nothing we can do to earn our salvation. Our salvation is purely a free gift of Grace from God for those who choose to accept it. Salvation is not a reward for behaving a certain way. It is a gift available to us through Jesus' actions on the cross (Ephesians 2:8-10).

If faith is belief that enables salvation and we can't do anything to earn salvation, then why did I define faith as "belief that results in action?" A simple question has a simple answer. Faith without good deeds is dead. John 3:19 describes actions as a result of belief. James adds that faith is dead if it lacks good deeds (James 2:14-17). In other words, good works are a byproduct of good faith. In elementary math, we learn simple input and output equations. If you input true faith, you'll get an output of good deeds. Jesus capitalizes on this premise when he speaks of good fruit in Matthew 7; "we know a tree by its fruit." If a tree produces bad fruit, it is a bad tree. If a tree produces good fruit, it is a good tree. What if the tree has produced no fruit when Jesus comes back and checks to see if it has been fruitful? It withers and dies (Matthew 21:19). It's similar to the parable where the master gives three servants bags of money. 2 of the servants invest it and double their money. One servant decides to bury it and give back the same amount given to him. When the master found out, he got upset and took the bag of money from the servant and gave it to the more prosperous servant. Jesus goes on, through the parable, to say, "if you do nothing with what you have, you will lose what little you have" (Matthew 25:29). Can somebody lose their salvation? Well, "we are saved by grace through faith" which means our salvation hinges on our faith. An individual can theoretically lose their faith by walking away from it, but they cannot lose their salvation. BUT, this does not mean that people who walk away are saved. To further explain this- if one has true faith, they won't lose it. Since true faith will not be lost, neither can salvation. Only those with false faith can lose it. Since it was false, they cannot lose the salvation that they never had to begin with. In other words, those who are saved will remain in faith.

In addition to faith, it's important to note that we can have faith of differing degrees. Jesus says in Matthew 17:20 that faith the size of a mustard seed can move mountains. This implies that we can have smaller (or larger) amounts of faith. Jude, a brother of Jesus, also describes Christians with wavering faith because of their doubt. There is a direct correlation between faith and doubt. Increased doubt decreases faith. If you want to increase your faith, start by decreasing your doubt.

Now that we've defined faith, we can define salvation. Salvation is an event, not a belief. Let me preface with that. Faith, which has a byproduct of repentance, is the belief that leads to salvation. To know what being saved is, we must first know what we are being saved from. In short, we all sin (Romans 3:23) and the wage of sin is death (Romans 6:23) which means that after we die we will stand before God and be judged. If we are saved, we will be saved from the punishment of our sins. If we aren't saved, we will pay the penalty for our sins. On judgment day, we are judged based on our thoughts and actions during our life. But this is what the gospel is all about! We are naturally born dead in our sin, deserving of the grave, but because of what Jesus did on the cross we can be made right in God's sight!

When we truly believe in Jesus and accept him into our hearts, the Holy Spirit dwells within us, and what was judgment day now becomes redemption day (Ephesians 4:30). On redemption day, all of our sins will be cleansed through Jesus' blood that was shed on the cross (1 John 1:7) so that we can enter heaven. So what is salvation? Our salvation is a two-part event: The event of salvation occurs after death but our salvation is enabled the moment we believe and have The Holy Spirit dwell within us. So we are saved at the moment of belief but salvation doesn't occur until after our death. Still, salvation occurs on redemption day because we are SAVED from our actions that deserve damnation.

We can discuss salvation now that we know what faith is and what impacts it. Salvation is a gift that we do nothing to earn, we only accept it through faith in Jesus Christ. As stated before, salvation is not earned; it is given. If there is nothing we can do to earn salvation, we can do nothing to lose salvation. Since faith can waver, people can choose to seemingly lose faith, but since salvation is given when we don't deserve it, we can do nothing to lose that salvation. This topic is often tricky and is divisive amongst many Christians. People will often quote verses in "support" of losing salvation, but in reality, it's talking about faith- not salvation. If somebody is genuinely saved (that is, they will be saved), then it is impossible for them to lose faith because, in order to be saved, they will have faith. It's a tricky subject because salvation is a future event that relies on current and future belief. Let's think about it this way- God exists outside of time. We can logically conclude this because He was, is, and always will be (Revelation 22:13). With that being said, God is all-knowing. He knows who is going to be saved on redemption/judgment day. If somebody is saved, that means they have a spot in heaven. However, if we could lose salvation, that would be the equivalent of plucking somebody directly out of heaven and throwing them to hell (in God's eyes) because of their actions. That is not biblical. Once we are in our destination after judgment, it is for eternity. The people that believe you can lose your salvation also believe they can receive salvation again. In God's eyes, this would be equivalent to somebody going back and forth from heaven and hell based on their own belief, resulting in action, coming and going as they please. That is not biblical. You are either saved, or you aren't. 1 John 2:19 says that if somebody leaves the church, it shows that they never truly belonged to the church. Hebrews 6:4-6 states, "For it is impossible to bring back to repentance those who were once enlightened— those who have experienced the good things of heaven and shared in the Holy Spirit, who have tasted the goodness of the word of God and the power of the age to come— and who then turn away from God. It is impossible to bring such people back to repentance; by rejecting the Son of God, they are nailing him to the cross once again and holding him up to public shame." So what does that mean? It means that you can't be saved twice. Why? Because if you're genuinely saved, what do you need saving from since you have already been saved?

Having authentic unending faith results in salvation. Just like in the Olympics, it is not how you start the race but instead how you end it (2 Timothy 4:7). End the race in faith. We aren't guaranteed tomorrow. Remember how faith results in action? Part of that action is repentance. So what is repentance? Like faith, repentance is a

Change of mind that results in a change of action (Acts 26:20). With that being said, to repent, in terms of salvation, means to change your mind regarding sin and Jesus Christ (Acts 2:38, Acts 3:19, Acts 17:30, Acts 20:21). When we repent, we are repenting from two things- The first is unbelief that Jesus died and was resurrected on the cross. The second is repentance from the actions of sin that we know we have committed. The ultimate sin is unbelief in Christ because that is what sends us to hell (John 3:18).

There will come a time in every Christian's life where we ask ourselves, "How do I know that I am saved?" It's among the most critical questions that we can ask ourselves. Here is how we answer it: Romans 10:9 says, "because, if you confess with your mouth that Jesus is Lord and believe in your heart that God raised him from the dead, you will be saved." So let me ask you a question; do you believe that Jesus is Lord, that He is God, and that God raised him from the dead? If you say "no," then you aren't saved. If you said yes, let me ask you this: Do your actions reflect what you believe? Our actions show that we belong to the truth (1 John 3:18-19). If we genuinely believe that Jesus died on the cross and was resurrected from the grave to save us from our sins, we will live for him. He died for us, so if we are genuinely saved, we will live for Him by walking in the spirit, not in the flesh. He died for us, so those who are saved (because they will be saved) will live for him.

Are you living for him? If you aren't sure what it looks like to walk in the spirit, ask yourself this question: do I show the fruits of the spirit? Galatians 5:22-23 says, "But the fruit of the Spirit is love, joy, peace, patience, kindness, goodness, faithfulness, gentleness, and self-control...." If you believe in Jesus and your life exemplifies the fruits of the spirit, I can guarantee you of your salvation. Don't expect perfection from yourself; God doesn't expect perfection from you. We know this because of the parable of the rich young man- Jesus says, "if you want to be perfect, go and sell all your things and give the money to the poor" (Matthew 19:21) but Jesus, being God, knew the rich young man wouldn't go and do it. God knows we aren't perfect, yet Jesus died for us anyway (Romans 5:8). I say that to say this, failure to exemplify all of the fruits of the spirit, all of the time, doesn't take God's gift of salvation through Jesus Christ away from you. Since you aren't perfect, you are expected to lack fruits occasionally. What's important is that your tree bears good fruit even though there may be some bad fruit with it. There's always a couple of bad apples, but make your new life (after accepting Jesus into your heart) a basket of good apples with only a few bruised ones.

Before I was a Christian, I did what I wanted to. I lived the way that I wanted. I sinned because I didn't care that it was a sin. However, once I found the faith, I recognized that my sin grieved God, so I changed my mind, which resulted in a change of actions. As best I can, I now live by what the Bible says. I repented when I decided to believe Jesus' actions saved me, which changed how I live my life. That is repentance. Repentance is not something that must occur after every sin so that we can be saved.

No. 1 John 1:7 says, *"for those who walk in the light, ALL sins are forgiven."* If you are saved, believe, and have repented, you are walking in the light. Do not be confused! Confessing our sins to God is incredibly important (1 John 1:9). As a result of salvational repentance, we will confess our sin as we become aware of it. Similar to how works are a byproduct of faith, confession of our sins is a byproduct of repentance. Many sins go unnoticed in our lives. Confess them as you learn them, but if you forget to confess because you were unaware of them or unable to confess them because you died, do not fret because you are still saved. God's grace and forgiveness are not progressive. He doesn't forgive us of our sins after we commit them. No, he forgave us of our sins long before we committed them. His grace does not hinge on your confession of every sin. His grace hinges on your repentant faith. For those who are saved, all of God's grace was made abundant on the cross- not after you confessed. If God's grace hinges on our repentant faith, what does repentant faith look like?

Chapter 9

Faith isn't easy

There aren't many guarantees in this lonely life. This dark and lonely world offers certain temporary comforts- instant gratification, status, people, things, sex, drugs, medication, and the list goes on and on. But, the more you entertain these things, the more it becomes like quicksand. With each waking moment that you partake, as you struggle more and more, it sucks you in beyond escape. It gets more accessible and easier to bounce from one addiction to the next and then circle your way back around to try them all again. The more you think about it, the more this world becomes meaningless. What level of fulfillment do the things of this world bring? It's as if we are a cup with a hole in the bottom. The world pours water into us, but our bottomless cup is left unsatisfied, so we constantly seek out more water sources.

Solomon said it best in Ecclesiastes: "Life is meaningless." Like Solomon, I've chased money, I've chased women, I've chased fulfillment in my work, I've chased the things that this world has to offer, but yet it's like chasing the wind, useless. In reality, this world offers fleeting pleasures that are tempting to chase. But, sadly, this is the only form of happiness they'll ever experience for most people. They'll revolve around alcohol like clockwork. They'll jump from pleasure to pleasure. But in the end, it doesn't matter what you do in this life because no matter who you are, what you saw, or what you did, you will return to dust just like the reprobate next to you. But that's just it. That is why faith is hard. Faith is hard because, with what this world has to offer, it's pointless. The world tells you there's no point to faith because the world has nothing to offer you. That's why we have faith in something out of this world. Faith is hard because it goes against the grain of the world, yet faith is fulfilling for that very reason.

I met my future wife only three months after God delivered me from my depression. I had abandoned the college that I wanted to go to and transferred to the college God had been nudging me towards. Within seven days, I met the girl who would bring light into my life for the rest of my days. Six months later, when I was 21 years old, I proposed. At the time, I was working as an Emergency Medical Technician (EMT), making only $34,000 a year. Though we were young and stupid, we were realistic enough to know it was hardly a liveable wage. Despite the world telling us not to get married, the judgemental comments, and the gossip within the church, we chose to rely on God.

After six more months, I had married my beautiful bride. I remember her walking down the aisle like it was yesterday. It was a sunny, early August afternoon. We were standing in front of a rustic barn with tall, wide wooden doors. The next thing I know, I'm standing front and center wearing a navy blue suit, a pink tie, brown suspenders, and brown shoes. Two hundred eyes are watching. My dad (the pastor) was standing at my 5 o'clock and my brother (best man) directly to my 9 o'clock. I was looking down at my feet, and the music changed- everything changed. I saw the grass-cut stone lined with white pews as I panned my vision upwards. Then, as the violinist played, I saw the only woman that mattered walking towards me. Her beautiful blonde hair was woven like a vine that God himself had created. Her upper dress was doused with lace as her lower was covered in clouds. As she strutted with her father towards me, I had to remind myself to smile because of how awe-inspiring she was. Then, a half-second later, the night was over, and I was driving off with my rib.

By getting married, we were going against the grain of this world, yet it was the most fulfilling thing I've ever done. According to the world, we were doing it all wrong- we had no money, no house, both in college and not even a good-paying job. Heck, it was a risk in our own eyes, but we knew it was what God wanted. However, knowing this aspect of God's plan doesn't make it easier. We had faith, and it was fulfilling. Having faith that God would provide was challenging, yet without fail, He did. Just as my wife and I had hope caused by young love, you have hope in knowing the character of God. He never fails. His love for you never fails. We may waver like a buoy in the ocean, but so long as we have faith in God, we'll remain anchored.

Faith isn't easy because we are promised persecution. Faith isn't easy because choosing to love God is a daily choice. Faith isn't easy because relationships aren't easy. Just as I put time into my spouse, I should want to put time into my relationship with God. Faith isn't easy because this world lacks faith. A life full of faith isn't easy because repentant faith requires a sacrificial life. Nothing easy in life is worth having; likewise, things you work hard for are only temporarily fulfilling. As a result of faith, our salvation is the only thing in this life that isn't temporary. It's eternal. Faith is the only thing we can actively invest in that has an everlasting outcome. High school economics teaches you to invest in a compounding interest account for retirement because it's worth the investment. You invest small amounts and reap no rewards for 40 or so years, and then when you retire, you have exponentially more than you put in. Our faith is similar. It is worth our time, money, and effort to invest in our retirement (eternal life) now without reaping any rewards in this life. Our faith enables us to have hope. When we have hope, it patches the bottomless cup that we are, and our cup will begin to overflow. Our world ignores the hole in the bottom of the cup and tries to fill us with different things but always fails. God recognizes the problem and patches the hole in our cup with Jesus Christ. Once we believe, our hole gets patched and we are able to finally be filled. Jesus, through his death and resurrection, gives us hope because the pain that you've been feeling can't compare to the joy that's coming. Once our patched cup of hope is full, God, the living water, will continually pour into us. Once we begin to overflow, we can begin to spread hope to others. Jesus told the woman at the well to "go and thirst no more" because he fills our every need. Jesus patches us right. But here's the honest truth: As our faith wavers, so does the level of hope in our cup. As we begin to backslide, we begin to lose faith. As we begin to lose faith, we begin to lose hope. As we begin to lose hope, we begin to lose motivation. Once we lose motivation, we are back to square one- nothing gets done, and life is meaningless. So to rejuvenate our wretched, lazy, unmotivated lives, we reinvest in our faith so that God can fill us up with hope yet again.

Find comfort in knowing you aren't alone. This is something that all Christians deal with our whole lives. In Matthew 13, Jesus tells parables of differing levels of faith. The parable of four soils is worth remembering- A farmer threw out some seed in his field. Some seeds fell on a path, and birds came and ate them; the seeds never even rooted. Some seeds fell on shallow soil with underlying rock. The seeds sprouted quickly but died because of their shallow roots. Some seeds fell among thorns, and they got choked out as they grew. Some seeds fell on fertile soil, and they later reaped a harvest. If you're anything like the disciples, you're wondering what this even means. Thankfully, Jesus explained it to us- The seeds on the path are those who hear God's message and reject it. The seeds on the rocky soil receive it with joy, but their flame quickly dies out. The seeds in the thorns are those who receive the word, but their faith gets choked out because of the pressures of this world. The seeds in fertile soil hear and receive God's word, thus producing a harvest. So I will label these the four levels of faith- path, shallow, thorn, and fertile. There are times when we bounce around in our faith, backslide, and change fields, but ultimately, what matters is that we end the race in faith. God knows our faith journey is a race; it doesn't matter how it starts, just how you finish. Those with proper faith produce a harvest according to Jesus- Are you producing harvest? If you are in a time of your life where you feel unfruitful (hateful, sorrowful, chaotic, impatient, rude, harsh, rotten, hopeless, and selfish), then you are not reaping a harvest. How do we reap a harvest? The fruits of the spirit are love, joy, peace, patience, kindness, gentleness, goodness, faithfulness, and self-control. Use these as a gauge to continually improve. We will not always be able to uphold all aspects of the fruit of the spirit, but as we grow in faith we will grow in fruit. Still, it should be an abnormality to be unfruitful.

Also, in Matthew 13, Jesus tells the parable of the mustard seed. Faith (the mustard seed) starts very small, but it becomes a huge tree where animals make their home when given proper nutrients. Unfortunately, Jesus doesn't give us an explanation of this parable. Still, if we care for our faith as the earth cares for the seeds, properly watering and nurturing the seed, our faith will become a beacon of hope for those around us. Sooner or later, our tree will drop seeds of its own into others' hearts, where their faith can begin to grow. That's the cycle of spreading faith! Seed, grow, then produce a harvest. Seed, grow, then produce a harvest. Hopefully, our tree will become bigger and bigger during this process, allowing for more and more creatures to have a beacon of hope.

Later in Matthew 13, Jesus tells us two more parables that are seemingly identical. In the first parable, Jesus says that a man discovers a treasure in a field that isn't his, so he goes and sells all his possessions to purchase the land. In the second parable, a merchant is looking for a valuable pearl, he finds one, and he goes to sell everything to purchase the pearl. At first glance, you think Jesus is telling the same point but with different parables. The first parable is about our faith, but the second is about God's love for us. When we find faith, it's not ours to have. We are broken sinners undeserving of

God's grace and mercy. However, through Jesus Christ, we can receive the gift of salvation by grace through faith. So we, like the man, should find Jesus (the valuable treasure), run, and get rid of everything hindering us from obtaining Jesus so that we can have Him. The Merchant is Jesus, he is looking for us, and once he found us, he gave everything to have us. Jesus, the merchant, wanted that pearl so bad that he was willing to die for us. Many more similar parables of faith are found throughout the gospel, like in Matthew 25. Still, it's important to remember that faith is like a tree. When appropriately nurtured, it grows, and once grown, it should bear fruit. Our faith should have fruit; if it doesn't, something is wrong. As we read in the previous chapter, faith without works is dead. It's not that works save us, but rather proper faith has a byproduct of good works. If an apple tree can't bear apples, what good is it?

If there's one point I'm trying to make with this chapter, it's this-Faith isn't easy but do not worry because you're not alone. All of our faith wavers, but we have to strive as hard as possible to ensure that we remain in faith. Our faith is the most important race we will ever run. Thankfully, it's a race for completion, not speed. Do you remember the comfort you felt in High School when your teacher said your grade was for completion? We should feel comfortable knowing that our faith is just a matter of completion. There aren't many guarantees that this world offers, but our God does offer many. One is that God can do the impossible, including saving you and me. The race of faith will be difficult. We will face persecution, financial troubles, people troubles, and be made fun of. Still, it will all be worth it when, in the blink of an eye, we stand before God in all of his glory, and he says, "well done, my good and faithful servant." When we stand before God, he will judge our sins if we aren't saved. If sins are so important, then what is sin? How do we sin? So why do we sin?

Chapter 10

"The Devil Made Me Do It"

It was a beautiful, windy fall afternoon. As I leaned my impatient red chubby cheeks against the smudged car window, I could see red cardinals fluttering in the air. My hands were itching with excitement, slowly tugging at the plastic surrounding my new toy. My mom would often take me with her on errand days, and as a consolation, she'd usually stop and get us lunch where I'd get a toy in my combo meal. There were some days when, for whatever reason, my mom would tell me to wait till I got home to open my toy. As you can imagine, I'd rush through my nuggets and plead, "Mommy, can I please play with my toy now?" As she would shake her head, "no," I'd throw my face to the window in hopes of finding entertainment while fiddling with the plastic encasing my toy. While looking out the window, I somehow managed to poke a hole through the plastic- I was in. Without my mom knowing, I had started playing with my toy prematurely. Knowing that my mom didn't want me to play with it, I stuck the toy back into the box as we pulled into the driveway.

Once we got inside, my mom checked to see if I ate enough, and she noticed that my toy was out of the packaging. She pulled me to the side and asked me, "Jared, did you open your toy after I told you not to?" I decided to lie, "No, Mommy. I didn't open it." She cocked her head with a raised eyebrow and said, "Did you just lie to me?" I doubled down, "No." Not long after my answer, I faced the wrath of discipline.

Why is it that I decided to lie at such a young age? I knew it was wrong to lie. I had been taught not to, but yet I did it anyway. Many people might say, "The Devil made me do it!" But is that realistic? No! The devil is not omnipresent. He cannot be in multiple places at once, which means if 100 people around the globe are saying it, 99 of them are wrong(but realistically, all of them are). I also think Satan has bigger fish to fry than dealing with Christians who are blaming every little sin on the devil; he has demons for that. Yes, people in biblical times and today get possessed by demons. While on the topic of spiritual warfare- it is real. The Bible says that we aren't at war against flesh and blood but against "principalities, against powers, against the rulers of the darkness of this world, and against spiritual forces of evil in the heavenly places" (Ephesians 6:12). If the devil has bigger fish to fry, who are his fish? My best guesses would be people of incredible influence- people capable of changing the world. Biblically, a person possessed by the devil was Judas, which occurred two separate times(Luke 22:3, John 13:27). If you think about it, Judas had amongst the most potential to change the world because of his relation to Jesus. Other big fish would include political figures, religious leaders, and seemingly insignificant people, like Judas, who Satan knows could change the world.

Why would Satan possess Judas rather than the other disciples? Because he was the easiest to manipulate (Judas had a love for money) and could change the world through Jesus. Satan knew the impact

Jesus could have, so he tried to stop it, using Judas as his vessel of destruction, but even Satan is under the will of God. I hold to this truth- intelligent people learn from their mistakes, but wise people learn from other people's mistakes. Looking at Judas' possession, we can learn how to conquer the devil. Ephesians 6 details the armor of God- Truth, Righteousness, Peace, Faith, Salvation, The Word of God, and Prayer. Using Judas as an example, the less consistent armor you have, the easier it is for the devil and his demons to manipulate you. So remain firm wearing the armor of God at all times, not putting down any aspect of the armor for any period of time.

Interestingly, there is another instance where Satan possibly possessed a disciple. Jesus called Peter "Satan" because Peter was essentially tempting Jesus not to die. Peter was selfish and didn't want Jesus to leave (Matthew 16:23). Why does this matter? Because Satan tempted Jesus with people that He loved. Though you may know you are firm in your faith and protected, Satan may use a loved one to manipulate you- it happens more often than you may think. So how do we avoid Satan's manipulation? We put on the armor of God and recognize that Satan only has the option to control our flesh because our spirit has been cleansed through Jesus. Our flesh isn't saved. It will die then decay. Our flesh is doomed, much like Satan, which is why God gave him the ability to control it. According to 2 Corinthians 12, we can conclude that Satan has the potential to place a demonic thorn in everybody's flesh because he put one in Paul's flesh. After all, Satan is the God of this world(2 Corinthians 4:4). The armor of God protects our spirit, but our flesh remains available for Satan, so what can we do to protect our flesh? Fasting. Fasting teaches us how to conquer our flesh. If we have control over our flesh, Satan has nothing to manipulate us with.

Allow me to clarify particulars. Judas was manipulated and possessed. This was before The Holy Spirit was made readily available for every believer, so Judas didn't have The Holy Spirit. His spirit was vulnerable. Spiritual possession is only possible if our spirit is vulnerable, which it is until we have The Holy Spirit. If we are saved then we have The Holy Spirit dwelling within us and our spirit is not vulnerable. However, fleshly manipulation can and does happen to everybody regardless of The Holy Spirit's presence. How is all of this possible? As humans, we have two natures- our flesh and our spirit. Paul describes the relationship between the two in Romans chapters 6-8. Have you ever felt like you want to do right, but you always manage to screw up? That's because the spirit knows best, but the flesh wins out. Paul says in Romans 7, "Though I want to do what is right, I inevitably do what is wrong." In context, Paul says our spirit wants to do right, but our flesh does wrong. It's a constant battle- Spirit v.s. Flesh. Why do we seemingly always fail, falling into temptation? There are many reasons, but they all narrow down to Satan. He initiated the fall of man, and to this day, he is ultimately responsible for the thorns in our flesh. What do those thorns look like? Sin and deprecating thoughts.

Paul says in 2 Corinthians 12 that a thorn was placed in his side, a demon, that kept him from becoming prideful. This means that he had a chip on his shoulder, something convincing him that he wasn't good enough... sound familiar? Paul wasn't possessed, but his thorn manipulated him. So if you have the Holy Spirit within you, Satan and his demons cannot possess you, but they can manipulate you through the flesh. The best way to tame your flesh is through fasting, but even then, you can't tame the flesh of loved ones. So be on guard. Our war is not against the flesh; it's against the powers and principalities of an unseen world. Fight for souls, not the protection of your flesh. Winning the flesh is a battle that each believer needs to win, but the greater war is spiritual.

I think that we often focus too much on our fruits. We strive to do good and solely focus on the good that we accomplish. Focusing on our fruits isn't a bad thing but we have to remember that a tree can only produce fruits if its roots are well nourished. The issue with focusing on fruits is that we'll forget to nourish our roots and our fruits will dry up. We have to nourish our roots! As a result of root nourishment, we will bear fruit. Our society is fruit driven and evidence based so it is easy to forget about our roots. Why am I saying this? Well, how do you dig up a tree? You uproot it. Satan doesn't waste his time attacking our fruits, no, he goes for our roots. So what are our roots? Our roots are our faith, relationship with God, reading the Bible, prayer, etc... That's why it is so hard to do these things consistently because Satan is attacking our roots. How can I lead others if I can't even lead myself? How can I teach others how to pray if I don't pray myself? My cup can't overflow if nothing is filling it. My tree can't grow if my roots lack nourishment. Give your roots nourishment! Invest in your relationship with God, making Him a priority, and Satan's army will struggle to dig up your roots.

When I was a child and I actively lied to my mom, did the devil make me do it? No. I chose it. Satan, through deceiving Adam and

63

Eve, made it an option but ultimately it was my choice. The same goes for you- you have a choice. Do you want to live by the flesh or the spirit- easily manipulated or firm in Jesus? It's a simple choice, but it's not easy. Like love, it is a choice to be made daily. Like marriage, a singular choice that you choose to make for the rest of your life. And like marriage and love, it can be the best choice you'll ever make.

Ultimately, we sin because we love our sin more than we fear our God. With each temptation we think to ourselves, "one time won't hurt" or "is it really that bad?" Then as we continue in sin, we begin to try and justify our sin. If we continue in this sin long enough, it will become routine. When sin becomes normal in your life, you are no longer walking in the spirit; you live in the flesh. If we are living in the flesh, we do not have the spirit of God in us, and we are not saved. Somebody who is saved WILL walk in the spirit. If you aren't walking in the spirit right now, seek genuine repentance. When we live in the flesh, we don't fear God enough. Somebody who isn't saved should be scared of God. God destroyed Sodom and Gomorrah quickly. God is the creator of all, and he has granted us life because of His love and mercy, but he can release his wrath on anybody at any time He chooses. So people who aren't saved should genuinely shake in their boots. Yet, they live in their flesh and have no fear of God. Those who are saved should not shake in our boots. That fear is replaced with Love and reverence for God. Perfect Love casts out all fear (1 John 4:18).

The Bible often speaks about fear, but one that sticks out is Proverbs 9:10, "The fear of The Lord is the beginning of wisdom." Many people associate fear with negative things, but fear is inherently good. God gave us fear to protect us. When in a dangerous situation, fear keeps us on edge and helps protect us. God gave us fear as a form of protection so when we have a fear of God it's a good thing. Some may look at fearing God as a bad thing, but I see it as something worth praising God for. Again, fear is inherently good. It is only when fear is abused that it becomes terrible. God will never abuse fear. The fear instilled in us by God is always a good thing because he is trying to protect us. When we read the book of Revelation or verses about Hell, we experience a healthy fear.

God gave us that fear to protect us from ourselves. All of the people who will experience God's wrath choose it. They actively choose to love their sin rather than God. It's an active choice, but actions have consequences like our mothers taught us. God won't abuse fear, but people can abuse the God-given fear. Be on the look out- Satan may be using another's flesh to lead you astray. With that being said, have you ever wondered why evil exists? Why does God allow Satan to manipulate our flesh?

Chapter 11

Why Does Evil Exist?

"Why does evil exist?" This is the question that has plagued the hearts of countless individuals. If we are honest with ourselves, it's a question that we have all probably thought, but it felt blasphemous even to ask. Is it okay to ask? Of course, it is! "If God is real, why is there evil in the world?"

It's pretty simple. Love. I recognize that sounds repulsive at first but hear me out. There is light and darkness in this world, hot and cold, good and evil. Without one, the other cannot exist. Because evil exists, there must therefore be good, and likewise, for there to be good in this world, there must also be evil. God allows evil in this world to recognize good when we see it. God is that Good. If God is good, that must make his adversary, the devil, the bad. Therefore, Satan is responsible for evil in this world. Naturally, we'll then ask, "Where did Satan get his evil from?" God created Satan with the same free will that He gave you and me. We know Satan has free will because 2 Timothy 2:26 says, "and they may come to their senses and escape from the snare of the devil, after being captured by him to do his will." In Satan's free will, Satan chose to rebel, thus enabling evil. Therefore, Satan is responsible for all evil- God simply allows it to happen so that you and I can spend eternity with him. As a result of

Satan's fall, you and I have the choice to choose to love God. Naturally, some people may say, "Well, God gave Satan the option of evil by giving him free will." But we have to remember that there is no love without free will. It's for that exact reason that God gave humanity free will because without it, we wouldn't have been free. We wouldn't have been truly loved. Yes, in that, I am saying that God inherently loves Satan because He gave Satan free will. God gave Satan free will knowing that Satan would abuse it and want to become God himself, but God did it anyway.

Why would God do that? Because God inherently loves Satan. But God despises evil, so he kicked Satan out of heaven. He loves the being of Satan, but he hates the evil of Satan. Think about it, God created everything and said it was good. This includes Satan. Jesus, being God, taught us to love our enemies (Matthew 5:44). God is not hypocritical. Jesus spoke out against the hypocritical Pharisees, so I believe God loves his enemy, Satan, just as He has asked us to do with our enemies. Also, consider this: why did God cast Satan to earth, knowing that satan would lead humanity astray? The only reason I can concoct, in accordance with the character of God, is that God loved Satan, so He gave Satan precisely what he wanted- a kingdom. Satan wanted to be God himself, so God gave Satan a kingdom to rule over. But obviously, God hates evil, and evil deserves to be punished. So God gave Satan a kingdom that was destined to be destroyed. After all, the Bible says that "Satan is the god of this world" (2 Corinthians 4:4). God gave Satan a kingdom of human inhabitants who God knew would choose to worship themselves rather than the king of their kingdom. God knew that humans, after the fall, would be selfish. God knew that they, as a whole, would be worshipers of self rather than worshipers of Satan. It's honestly the genius of God at hand. How? By giving Satan his kingdom, he simultaneously shows his superiority (because all the Heavens know Satan will fail) while giving humanity the ability of free will and creating genuine love between God and humanity. So because Satan is on earth, we have free will.

Because we have free will, we can choose to love God. Because we can choose to Love God, we create a marital relationship rather than a master and slave type relationship. Because of free will, we can choose to marry God rather than be forced to Love God, which God wanted all along. He allowed Satan's fall so that He could love us properly. So because evil exists, we can have a relationship with God in a loving, consensual marriage. When writing this chapter, I asked God to speak to me if he wanted to add anything else, and he led me to the book of Habakkuk.

In the book of Habakkuk, Habakkuk cries out to God in desperation. Evil surrounds him, yet God is seemingly nowhere, so he says, "where are you?" (Habakkuk 1:1-4). Then God responds and says, "Look and be amazed...I am doing something in your own day, something you wouldn't believe...I am raising Babylonians, a cruel and violent people. They will march across the world and conquer other lands... their charioteers charge from far away" (Habakkuk 1:5-8). So amid Habakkuk's clouded judgment, God was building the solution beyond Habakkuk's perspective. God knew the hearts of the evil Babylonians and planned to use their free will to destroy the wicked people that Habakkuk was worried about. God uses humanity's free will to accomplish His will. After hearing that his country would be conquered, Habakkuk naturally responded, what about us? " Habakkuk says, "...Surely you aren't going to wipe us out... you are pure and cannot stand the sight of evil...will you let them get away with this..." (Habakkuk 1:12-17)? To which God responds, "Look at the proud! They trust in themselves, and their lives are crooked. But the righteous will live by their faith...they [the proud and wealthy] open their mouths as wide as the grave, and like death, they are never satisfied...But soon, their captives will taunt them...debtors will take action. They will turn on you [the proud and wealthy] and take all you have..." (Habakkuk 2:4-7). So God is essentially saying to Habakkuk that the righteous will live by their faith. He will use the oppressed to overcome the oppressors to not get away with their wickedness. In a prayer of thankfulness, Habakkuk cries out to God, "I am filled with awe by your amazing works... in your anger, remember your mercy...His [God] coming is as brilliant as the sunrise. Rays of light flash from His hands, where His awesome power is hidden. Pestilence marches before Him; plague follows close behind...He is the Eternal One...was it in anger, Lord, that you struck the rivers and parted the sea [referring to saving ancient Israelites]? Were you displeased with them [ancient Israelites]? No, you were sending your chariots of salvation" (Habakkuk 3:2-8)! Habakkuk is praising God and listing reasons why he is worthy of praise, but did you notice how he praised God for being amid pestilence and plagues? Usually in hard times we blame God for the bad things happening to us, but Habakkuk is praising God for them because he knows that God is in their midst! That is what faith looks like! Then, Habakkuk recalled when God delivered ancient Israel from Egypt. He remembered that the Egyptian chariots chasing after Israelites, a seemingly bad thing, ended up being the method of salvation that God used to free them from the Egyptians. At this moment, I strongly encourage you to reflect on your life. Please think of the seemingly bad events that have happened to you: death, financial hardship, rejection, whatever it may be. Then ask yourself this question: "Was that God's method of salvation for me?" The answer is yes. You are where you are today because of the hard things you have faced. All of these bad things that have happened to you weren't God showing you His anger. It was God delivering you! Once Habakkuk realized this, he says, "I trembled inside when I heard this; my lips quivered with fear... even though the fig trees have no blossoms, and there are no grapes on the vines; even though the olive crop fails, and the fields lie empty and barren; even though the flocks die in the fields, and the cattle barns are empty, yet I will rejoice in the Lord! I will be joyful in the God of my salvation! He makes me surefooted as a deer, able to tread upon the heights" (Habakkuk 3:16-19). Hard times are scary! God told Habakkuk that hard times were coming just like you and I know that hard times will come. Yet, despite those hard times, Habakkuk says, "I will rejoice in the Lord" (Habakkuk 3:18). I urge you all, with every ounce of my being, to be joyful in the God of our salvation even though chariots are riding our way. Be joyful in the God of our salvation even though war surrounds us. Be joyful in the God of our salvation even though death, pestilence, and plagues are among us. Be joyful in the God of our

71

salvation, resting in his embrace, because this is God's method of salvation for us.

Some may think, "If God utilizes evil, then that makes him immoral!" Actually, not in the slightest. According to philosophy, it makes him more moral. There's a classic philosophical idea to prove this, and it's called the trolley problem. It goes something like this- You are the operator of a trolley/train. You are riding on the tracks, and then the track splits. You can't stop the trolley because it has to keep going. You have one person on one track, and on the other, you have 20 people. Because you can't stop- you have to choose.

Which track do you go down? No question. You kill the 1 to save the life of 20. And that's considered a moral decision. God has the same decision except with evil- one track allows evil on earth and saves some humans; the other track is the eternal damnation of all people in history. It's an obvious choice! God chooses to allow evil so that all people can be saved if they so choose. "Well, why can't God, if he's all-powerful, just stop the train?" He could, but we would no longer have free will if he did. Again, if we don't have a choice, then there's no free will, and if there's no free will, there is no true love. So for us to have free will, that trolley/train has to continue on the track.

There's another way to explain the "immorality of God". I don't know that it has a name, but I think it's incredibly beneficial in understanding God. When a gardener creates a garden, he gives it boundaries and knows what he wants to plant. Let's assume this gardener wants to grow a prized rose bush amongst a few other things. Over time, that rose bush starts to grow, so the gardener placed parameters on it: don't grow higher or wider than this. If the rose bush grew beyond the parameters, the gardener would trim the bush back to size. But, like any garden, weeds found a way to creep in, so the gardener plucked the weeds because they were a threat to his prized rose bush. Why do we blame God for plucking the weeds but not the gardener? In this parable, God is the gardener. God's children are the prized rose bush, and wickedness is the weeds. In the beginning, God created the perfect garden for his prized rose bush. But, over time, the rose bush began to grow beyond the gardener's set parameters. His children began to sin and stray from his word. So, he trimmed the bush. He trimmed, or corrected, his children by giving them the law. We see the gardener plucking weeds throughout the Old Testament to protect the rose bush from the weeds.

One time, the garden was so overrun with weeds that the gardener flooded the whole garden to protect the rose bush. It nearly wiped out the rose bush, but the gardener knew it wouldn't wipe it entirely out. It was drastic, but that's what he chose to do because that was best. Nowadays, both the weeds and rose bush have the law written on our hearts (Hebrews 10:16). Is it right for the rose bush or the weeds to place the exact boundaries and parameters of the garden on that of the gardener who exists outside of the garden? No! Is it right for people to judge God by the law he has given us for this life even though he exists outside of where the law applies? Of course not!

So why does evil exist, and why is God not evil? Evil has to occur so that we can choose to love God and spend eternity in paradise. God isn't evil because he is the epitome of perfect morality since he is the being that exists outside of the morality that he has specifically given to us for the time being. God allows evil so that His love can be evident and deliver you toward salvation.

Chapter 12

God's Existence

Before I met my wife, a girl I had met invited me to go on a stargazing date. I didn't know anything about her other than that she had my attention. This was right after I got out of my depression. I had only recently begun pursuing God, so I was vulnerable to temptation. I knew better, but I didn't KNOW better. We agreed to just go on a typical "dinner and walk around downtown" date. I went to her house to pick her up, enjoyed the date, and took her home, but she asked me to wait outside as I was dropping her off. This intrigued me. In all my years past, no girl had ever asked me to wait outside after I dropped her off, so I waited. The next thing I know, she comes out with pillows and a blanket, grabs me by the hand, and says, "Come on! Follow me!" I was dazed and confused but not stupid. I knew what she was planning, but I didn't know what words to say, so I went with her.

I blinked and was surrounded by a forest. It was a Midsummer night, owls hooting in the distance, full moon, and stars shining. It was a gorgeous night. She had taken me to a new, vacant log cabin with an open deck on top of the house. As we reached the top, I saw what she was planning. She had lined dim lights around the porch railings and laid the pillows and blankets down. I knew what she wanted, but I was too dumb to leave. I was still just curious. As she laid down, I glanced around and saw a gorgeous moon-lit mountain view. Before your mind starts to wonder, nothing happened. She asked me to lay down with her, and after about an hour and a half, I did sit down, and about an hour and a half later, I laid down. As we were lying there, looking up at the stars, she asked me, "So what do you think about all of this? Do you ever think about the universe and where we came from?"

I was shocked. I knew she wasn't a christian, so I wondered where she was going with this. I responded, "I don't so much wonder anymore. God works wonders." Without surprise, she said, "Hmm. Yeah." And I said, "Do you believe in God?" to which she calmly responded, "I wouldn't necessarily say I believe in God, but I am spiritual and believe that there's something bigger out there." Our conversation didn't last long because she had other things on her mind. At this point, she had told me enough about herself to where I was no longer romantically interested. Still, I stayed until 4 a.m. because she was a good friend.

I've always been a fan of stargazing for date ideas. It's a great excuse to talk and get to know the depths of a person, but as I've gotten older, I have realized that stargazing comes with temptations. A month or two later, my wife and I agreed to go stargazing on our first date. I had gone on stargazing dates before, so I knew what to do, what not to do, where to go, and when to go. I learned of the temptations associated with stargazing in the bed of a cozy pickup truck and on a rooftop deck, so I knew to flee from that possibility. Still, I also knew this girl was different. I knew I didn't want to do anything that would jeopardize our potential relationship. We were in the mountains of North Georgia; there was a cool, gentle, end of August breeze. We had been on our date for a few hours when we arrived at a public lookout spot. I'm not a native to that area, but I imagine it's where all the teens go to make regrets. Because I didn't want to tango with temptation, so I didn't bring pillows, blankets, or anything comfy.

We got out of the car and sat on the warm hood. We were overlooking a vast mountain landscape, but it was a bit foggy out. It wasn't long before we began to look up. She started pointing out various constellations and calling them by their names. I was intrigued. No girl had ever done that before. The last girl I had dated taught me not to give my attention to just anyone. But this girl astonished me with her knowledge and beauty. She'd be pointing into the sky, and I'd find myself glancing over at her in amazement. She didn't just have my attention; she captivated me. As we sat there talking about life, our necks began to hurt, so we decided to lay down in the uncomfortable asphalt parking lot. It wasn't long before we started talking about God. I remember asking her deep theological questions just to see what she thought. I honestly don't remember her answers, but they must've been right because we made our relationship official that night, and now I'm married to her!

When people visit a museum with beautiful art, they ask themselves, "Who painted this?" When we listen to a song we like, we ask ourselves, "Who sings this?" When we look at a beautiful creation, like stars, it's only reasonable to ask ourselves, "Who or what did this?' But why do we ask of a creator? Because it is logical to look at the creation and wonder of its creator. In neither of those situations was the conversation of God forced; they both naturally came up. Is it possible that if we surround ourselves with man-made objects, we will begin to view ourselves as gods? On the contrary, is it possible that if we surround ourselves with divinely made objects, we will begin to understand that there is a higher divine being? The environment you put yourself in shapes who you become and what you believe.

There are many kinds of people, but we can split everybody into three groups: Atheist (there is no god), Agnostic (there might be a god), and Deist (there is a god or gods). It's important to know what these terms mean because how we approach the conversation differs. If I'm talking to somebody who believes in a god, I don't have to prove his existence to them. However, If I'm talking to an atheist, I have to first prove a creator's existence before showing them how that creator is the biblical God. There's more nuance to it, but you get the point. If we are trying to share the gospel with an atheist, we must first convert them to an agnostic. Once they are agnostic, we can show them how God exists and why He is the one true God.

One day, a coworker recommended that I check out Ligonier Ministries. If you aren't familiar, the ministry was started by R.C. Sproul who is a big name in Christianity. While driving from work to my girlfriends' house, I started listening to R.C. Sproul. In one of his sermons, he mentioned his logical argument for the existence of God. The argument goes something like this: there are four ways things come into existence. Something is either eternal, an illusion, appeared spontaneously or was created. For example, let's look at a pen. Is a pen eternal? Has it always existed from the beginning of time? No, of course not. That would be absurd. If it's not eternal, then maybe it's an illusion. But we have all held pens before, and pens can write- they have a verifiable purpose and leave evidence of their existence after being used. So pens aren't an illusion. If it's not an illusion, then maybe it spontaneously appeared! After all, we didn't see it come off the factory conveyor belt, so it may be that it just spontaneously appeared. Logically, pens aren't spontaneously created. There are even people that work in pen factories that can confirm this conclusion. If we are intellectually honest with ourselves, we all know pens don't spontaneously appear because they are created, manufactured, then shipped out. If that's the case, that must mean that pens are created.

Why am I rambling on about pens? Because this line of questioning can be attributed to everything- trees, birds, people, food, and even God Himself. Trees aren't eternal, aren't an illusion, and don't spontaneously appear, which means the most logical option is that trees were created. What about God? God is eternal. We don't have to continue with the line of questioning because he fits the first categorical question. Almost every atheist I've come across is a believer in science. There has only been one atheist that didn't affirm every aspect of evolution, but that's because he was intellectually dishonest. He only used evolution when it aligned with his argument. Which, by the way, if you plan on talking with an atheist, make it a priority to ask them, "If I could prove to you that God exists and it was undeniable, which I'm not saying I can, but if I could, would you worship Him?" If they say "No," then continue at your discretion, but

I advise you not to waste your time. Very rarely do atheists say "yes" to that question. If somebody isn't willing to worship God, it doesn't matter what they believe about God because they'd be equal to the demons- and we know their fate (James 2:19).

Therefore, with logic alone, we can verify the existence of a creator. What other non-biblical evidence do we have? Until this point in the book, I've only given scriptural references in the parenthesis next to my claim. In this chapter, after I make a claim, you'll see a number in those parentheses that corresponds to the source found at the end of the chapter. This chapter has already discussed why a creator must exist through logic alone. The remainder of this chapter will describe the scientific, philosophical, mathematical, and historical pieces of evidence that suggest a creator and, ultimately, the God of the Bible. To show the evidence of God, we must first agree that there is a creator. What is the scientific evidence for this claim? For the sake of memorization, remember the acronym T.U.R.G.N. I want to point out that T.U.R.G.N. isn't evidence for a creator. Instead, its purpose is to exploit modern belief and then provide a new flawless belief system at the end. This is surface-level knowledge. I implore you to dive deeper into your own studies.

The "T" stands for "Thermodynamics," as in the "First Law of Thermodynamics," which states that energy cannot be created nor destroyed(1). In grade school, we are all taught that the universe began with a big bang. The going theory is that the Big Bang began through quantum fluctuations (2). However, by definition, quantum fluctuations require energy input to occur (3). So, if Quantum fluctuations instigated the big bang and quantum fluctuations require energy to function, where did the fluctuation receive its energy from? So essentially, science says "energy" created the big bang. To an extent, I agree. I just think that "energy" has a few more eternal characteristics like all-knowing, all-powerful, and all-present. Quantum fluctuations are interesting because, to occur, they have to violate the first law of thermodynamics (3).

The "U" stands for "Universe" as in "The Universe is expanding" (4). Still, something has to have a place of origin for it to expand. That's logical. Science agrees; that's where The Big Bang comes into play. As children, we were all taught that the universe is infinitely big, but here's the flaw with modern science- if the universe is infinite, it can't expand. Infinity can't grow beyond infinity.

The "R" stands for "Radiation Afterglow." Residual afterglow is the residual heat of creation; in other words, it is the afterglow of the big bang streaming through space (5). The quantum fluctuation that caused the big bang, an explosion, put off an extensive amount of heat. That heat is still trackable through radiation afterglow. This proves that the universe was not and is not infinite because we can track it from its beginning. From the Christian perspective, when God spoke, He brought forth life. This resulted in heat being created through energy, which resulted in creation.

The "G" stands for "Great Galaxy seeds," which aren't sci-fi. Believe it or not, they are bundles of matter, seeds of galaxies that just so happen to be a perfect size (6). Like a flower has seeds, these are seeds but for galaxies. If they were any smaller, they would dissipate. If they were larger, the new galaxy wouldn't be capable of sustaining itself because it would collapse (6). On top of that, there's seemingly nothing keeping these Galaxy seeds from getting smaller or bigger. If there is no lid to the container in an infinite universe, it'll infinitely expand. Likewise, if nothing contains a galaxy seed, it'll grow or shrink infinitely (6). This necessitates an intelligent designer because the universe would collapse on itself if there weren't a force acting upon it.

The "N" stands for "Newton," as in "Newton's first law of motion." If you aren't familiar, it is the theory that states, "An object at rest will stay at rest, and an object in motion will stay in motion at a constant velocity unless acted upon by an unbalanced force" (7). So how does this apply? Space is a vacuum, and it has no friction(8). Therefore, if the universe is expanding, it must have always been in motion UNLESS something instigated the change. Atheists may respond, "Yeah, the big bang initiated the change." BUT, at the beginning of the universe, the Big Bang, if objects at rest stay at rest, the objects responsible for The Big Bang would have remained at rest UNLESS something instigated it. In other words, the energy levels that instigated the quantum fluctuations which resulted in the big bang would have remained the same unless something instigated the change. This means that something caused the energy levels to change which resulted in the quantum fluctuations which caused the big bang. So what? It means that all objects in motion have to have an origin. Even the subtle quantum fluctuations have to have an origin because nothing can move unless instigated by an outside force.

Therefore, whatever created space and time must be spaceless, timeless, and immaterial because space and time cannot create themselves. This is evident because space and time haven't always been in motion and must have had something to instigate it. This means that Christians ought to believe that God is spaceless, timeless, and immaterial. Three attributes of God that you may be more familiar with that encompass those three attributes: omniscient, omnipotent, and omnipresent.

We've all heard it- "if we were slightly closer to the sun, we'd die, and if we were slightly further, we'd freeze to death." Earth spins at a rotation of 24 hours; if it spun faster or slower, we would all fly off into space or be crushed by the gravitational force of the earth. Earth's axial tilt is 23.4 degrees, perfectly between its two extremes (9). We would either burn or freeze to death if it were slightly off. The earth is "fine-tuned" for our existence perfectly. In other words, we are on the perfect ball, in the perfect place, in the perfect location, in the perfect galaxy, and in the perfect spot in the universe to sustain life.

Mathematically, the probability of this occurring randomly is statistically impossible. Let's not forget that this perfect order came from a rapid, chaotic expansion. By the way, since when does order result from chaos without any instigation? It doesn't. Something instigated the order amidst the chaos. This objection to modern belief is called the "fine-tuning argument." I strongly encourage you to study it yourself.

In summary, the fine-tuning argument lays out the probability of life. It recognizes that there must be a cause for existence. Here are three key points to remember:

1. If the universe began to exist, then it has a cause of its beginning.

2. The universe began to exist.

3. Therefore, the universe has a cause of its beginning.

This parallels the "Law of Causality," which states that everything has a cause for its existence. Since the Big bang occurred, it had a cause. That cause had to be instigated, or determined, by something that existed before the big bang. I strongly encourage you to study "the fine-tuning of the universe" more in-depth to develop your understanding further.

Recently, the popularization of "multiverses" has introduced us all to the idea of different possible worlds. For example, in the early 2000's we only had one spider man- Tobey Maguire. But now, Marvel has introduced us to three spider-men. They are all spider-man, but they all exist in different worlds. With multiverse theory, there's a possibility that there is a world where spider-man does exist. So what's the point? I'm introducing you to the ontological argument. The Ontological Argument is essentially "If God possibly exists, then God exists." The Oxford dictionary defines the ontological argument as "the argument that God, being defined as most great or perfect, must exist, since a God who exists is greater than a God who does not." Let's keep it simple. Here are the 6 points of progression: 1) It's possible that a maximally great Being exists. 2) A maximally great Being exists in some possible world. 3) If a maximally great Being exists in some possible world, it exists in every possible world (like spider-man in the marvel universe). 4) If a maximally great Being exists in every possible world, it exists in the actual world. 5) A maximally great Being exists in the actual world. 6) Therefore, a maximally great Being exists. A maximally great Being would be defined as a Being that isn't constrained by anything (omnipotent), any place (omnipresent), or any information (omniscient). Again, I strongly encourage you to study this further.

Can we be good without God? You're probably thinking, "Yes. People who aren't christian do good deeds all the time," but that doesn't answer the question. The question is, "Are we capable of good without God?" This is called "The Moral Argument." It essentially states that if God does not exist, then objective moral values do not exist. This means if we can prove the objectivity of morality, then we can have evidence for God. Think of it like this- when somebody gets trapped in an avalanche, they lose their reference point. They get tossed and tumbled and become encased by white snow. They have no clue what is up or what is down. From their point of view, down could be in any direction (subjective truth), but we all know that there is objective truth- down is down. Similarly, we have some objective morality, but many people think everything is subjective. If there is no God, there is no objective reference point. If there is a God, there is an objective reference point. Since we know that down is down (a reference point), we know there is a God. So let's relate this to morality instead of an analogous avalanche. In our culture, we can all agree that murder is objectively wrong. There is no debate. If morality is subjective, then murder would be permissible. But perhaps this only applies to our culture? No. Throughout history and the world, murder has been morally wrong. Murder was even wrong in cultures that had no contact with one another in the early years of human history. This means that we all have a reference point, a down is down, of morality. If murder, as an example, doesn't float your boat because sometimes it is permissible, like in times of war, then substitute it with greed or abuse. But those are objectively bad things; there are also objectively good things, such as generosity and sacrificial love for one another. All of which can be used to show that there is objective morality. Where does that objective morality come from? The going theory, which is valid to an extent, is that we are a product of our environment. From the moment we are born, the world around us (people, places, experiences, words, etc.) shapes us into who we are today. Regarding morality, we learn what is right and wrong predominantly from those who raise us- parents or legal guardians. But where did they learn their morals from? Their parents. Where did they learn their morals from? Their parents. Keep asking, "Where did it come from," and sooner or later, you'll trace it back to the first people. Then we ask one more time- "where did right and wrong come from if we learn right and wrong from our parents?" From my experience, this is where responses get illogical and shifty. People will say anything other than admit that something taught the first people right and wrong. For example, they'll say, "they just knew. What was wrong harmed their community and what was right benefited them most." But here's the flaw in that- human nature is selfish. Inherently, we don't do things for the good of our community. We do things that are good for ourselves because we are inherently selfish. We only do good things for others when we are TAUGHT to do good for others. Think of a toddler- they are inherently selfish, screaming, "that's mine! I want this!" Toddlers only learn to share and help others when their parents teach them to share. So it doesn't make sense that the original humans would do what was right for their community unless they were taught not to be selfish. In Christianity, we believe that God walked with Adam and Eve and instructed things to do and things not to do- he instructed them on right and wrong. Our morality is not subjective, we learn it from something capable of teaching us. Since morality is objective, it requires a being above humanity to determine right and wrong. Again, I strongly encourage you to study the moral argument further.

Have you ever asked yourself, "Why does math work?" Mathematics is something that we are taught from a young age, and we often forget that it occurs all around us naturally. The more you think about it, the crazier the idea of math working in all applications becomes. If the big bang occurred without a cause, then the bang was chaotic. If this universe exists by chance, how is it possible that the order of mathematics exists throughout the chaos? Paul Davies, a physicist affiliated with the institute for quantum studies for Chapman University in California, once said, "Mathematics is universal. It's discovered by human beings, but the rules of mathematics are the same throughout the universe and the laws of the universe."

Logically, order never derives from chaos. However, a "Chaos Theory" states that order can result from chaos if given infinite time and randomness. As you dive deeper into this theory, this randomness can only occur if it receives an energy input. Do you see where I'm getting at? Where does this energy come from in the case of the chaotic big bang? To answer scientifically, I think God supplied the energy to the chaotic big bang, which resulted in the order of the universe. So to answer the question of "Why does math work?" People will say, "Since the universe has an order, mathematics applies." But I think it is the other way around. I think that because Mathematics applies, the universe has order. Either way you look at it, the universe has order which means something created the universe with order. Order is not spontaneous and requires an energy input to form. Therefore, God created the universe with mathematics, so we have order throughout the known universe. Galileo Galilei, an Italian mathematician, astronomer, and philosopher, once said, "Mathematics is the language in which God has written the universe," and I couldn't agree more. As evidence of my claim that God made the universe with Mathematics, I bring forth the Fibonacci sequence, a.k.a. The Golden Ratio. The Golden Ratio is often called "The fingerprint of God" as well as "The Divine Ratio." Look at the pictures below.

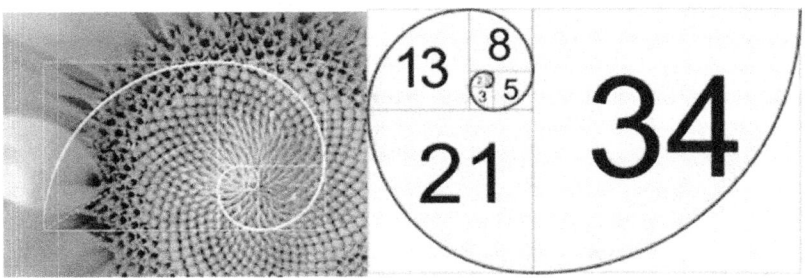

The Fibonacci sequence, according to the Oxford Dictionary, is a "series of numbers in which each number (Fibonacci number) is the sum of the two preceding numbers. The simplest is the series 1,

1, 2, 3, 5, 8, etc." When depicted, it forms a spiral shape. This spiral shape is depicted throughout nature; hence, it is called "The Fingerprint of God" because God has left his fingerprints on his creation.

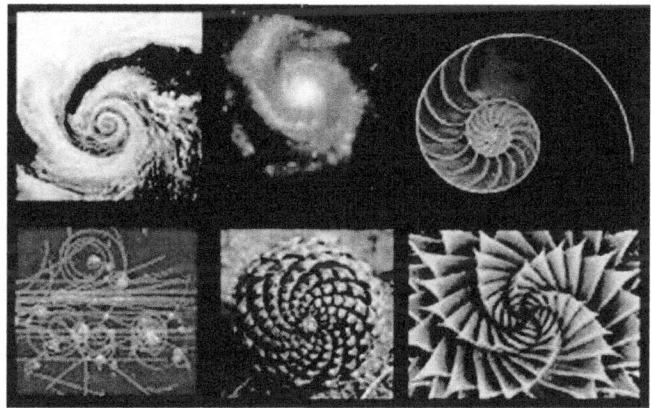

The evidence of a creator is creation. The Fibonacci sequence is found throughout creation. Here are some examples of where we observe the Fibonacci sequence naturally: Fetus', Galaxy's, Roses, Fists, Sunflowers, Fingerprints, and many others.

How is this evidence of a creator? It shows order and design. Some might argue that through evolution, plants adapted over time to form these shapes because they were the most efficient for photosynthesis. But this is quickly debunked. There is no fossil of a plant with the Fibonacci sequence today that didn't have it previously in its ancestral fossil record. I challenge you to try and find one. Plus, that refutation attempt doesn't debunk the other natural occurrences, only plants. The Golden Ratio is also found in our human D.N.A.

Charles Darwin, the father of evolution, claimed cells to be a gelatinous body that builds off each other in his book "on the origin of species." He was essentially claiming that our bodies are cells of gelatin that continuously build off one another to form our bodies. He was wrong. Our cells are so much more complex than that. Each factory within the cell was created for a purpose. Nowadays, these purposes are taught in grade school, and we understand them further because of D.N.A.

Your mind is blown right now if you're anything like me, but we are just getting started. Human D.N.A. contains a complex language system. It has grammar, punctuation, linguistics, spell check, alphabet, algorithms, etc. It is the most complex language known to man. Yet, it somehow managed to create itself through evolution? What if I told you that our human D.N.A. has a creator, and that creator signed his name on our D.N.A.? For context, in Exodus chapter three, God reveals his name to Moses. In Hebrew, the language spoken and written for the old testament, God's name is "YHWH." It is spelled out for pronunciation as "Yahweh."

In human D.N.A., there are four nucleotide base pairs-Adenine, Guanine, Thiamine, Cytosine. There is also a Sulfuric bridge that holds aspects of the D.N.A. strand together. This sulfuric bridge occurs every so often in a repeatable sequence. It occurs after 10 nucleic acids have been placed, 5 nucleic acids, after 6, and after 5. This process continually repeats (10). For simplicity, the numerical value of the sulfuric bridges is 10-5-6-5. Here is where it gets interesting, the biblical name for God (YHWH) contains the exact numerical values in the ancient Hebrew- yo(10) he(5) vav(6) he (5). So the order of 10, 5, 6, 5 translates to Hebrew as Y, H, W, H. Our D.N.A. has YHWH's name written within it. Science proves that our body repeatedly praises YHWH. This is incredibly interesting because all of the earth praises God (Psalm 66:1-4), even without them realizing it. I wouldn't consider that evidence of anything but it's interesting, don't you think?

I stated earlier that to convince an atheist of THE God, they must first be convinced of A god. I also stated the purpose of this chapter is "to exploit modern belief and then provide a new flawless belief system at the end." Up until this point, I've only revealed the flaw of modern belief and provided you with evidence for A god. If you have any rational mind, this is enough evidence for you to recognize that we are not here by accident. We were designed and created for a purpose. Here's the truth: Evidence is relative. Some people could read one previous paragraph and feel that it is sufficient evidence to believe in a god. Others would have to read this whole chapter, study it themselves, concoct counterpoints, and then believe there is A god. Still, others will concoct counterpoints and then produce counter-counter points and the evidence will never be enough.

My point is this, evidence, by itself, is not proven, and the amount of evidence needed to prove God is relative per person. For some, little evidence is proof. But for others, it can never be proven. In my subjective opinion, this is sufficient enough evidence to prove that there is A god. Romans 1:18-20 states, *"For the wrath of God is revealed from heaven against all ungodliness and unrighteousness of men, who by their unrighteousness suppress the truth. What can be known about God is plain to them because God has shown it. His invisible attributes, namely, his eternal power and divine nature, have been clearly perceived, ever since the creation of the world, in the things that have been made. So they are without excuse."* In other words, what I have provided should be sufficient enough evidence for all to prove that a god exists. If this isn't enough evidence, then I fear they will never find sufficient evidence and die apart from God. What I have written thus far proves the existence of a creator, not that it is the biblical God. So now we have the evidence to convert an atheist to agnostic, but why Christianity? So how do we prove the existence of THE biblical God?

If you grew up in Sunday school as a child, you've heard of Noah's flood. The biblical flood account is found in Genesis 6-9. To summarize, God had good reason to flood the earth and destroy all living creatures (Non-Christians will strongly oppose this). This flood came with tons of rain as they had never seen. Because of his love for humanity, God found one righteous man named Noah and decided to save him and his family from the flood. Some believe the flood to be regional, but I believe it was a worldwide flood because God said he would destroy every living thing (Genesis 6:13). Do history and archeology affirm this worldwide flood? I believe so. Marine fossils have been found high up Mount Everest (11). Yes, marine organism fossils have been discovered on Mount Everest, the highest elevation on earth (~29,000 feet above sea level). But science has a rational answer to this: The summit of Everest used to be on the seafloor 470 million years ago (12). But how do they know that? Because the fossils they found existed in the ocean 470 million years ago. Therefore, they theorize the summit of the world's tallest mountain is 470 million years old. Yet, the mountain is 60 million years old (13). At first glance, that seems like a contradiction. Still, there is a simple answer-the limestone found at the summit existed long before the tectonic plates shifted to create the mountain. But it still doesn't sit right with me. They dated the limestone on the summit to 470 million years because that's when those fossilized organisms lived. So how did they date the fossilized organisms? To date the fossil, they date the rock (14) around it. In other words, they date the fossils because of the rock, and they date the rock because of the fossils. This is very circular and unreliable. Yes, this scientific theory makes sense with the narrative they created, but what if there were a better theory? People can argue my point all day long but get this, during my research, I found a study that proves a "large monsoon" swept through the Himalayas. In this study, they say, "the existence of glacial advances during times of increased insolation suggests that enhanced moisture delivered by an active south Asian summer monsoon is largely responsible for glacial advances in this part of the Himalaya" (15). In simpler terms, a vast storm brought tons of water that washed through the Himalayas. Personally, a proven monsoon sweeping through the Himalayas (where Mount Everest is located) and depositing dead animals, later to be called fossils, is a more believable story than the current "circular reasoning" narrative.

Did you catch the similarities between the "monsoon" and what is described in the Bible? This "monsoon" coupled with the marine fossils on Everest is only a piece of evidence when proving the biblical flood. Is there more to support the worldwide biblical flood? Yes. Archeologists have found saltwater marine organisms in Kansas (16). How did it get there? Because they found the fossil there, science theorizes the ocean once went that far inland. This is the only logical thing in their mind, so it's considered a fact. This means the fossil is the evidence for their narrative, which is circumstantial at best, but again, what if there was another theory- a better theory? A theory that matches other proven archaeological and historical finds? Better yet, this theory has multiple groups of people that attest to it- the worldwide flood theory. Cedarville University published a study on the worldwide flood accounts across multiple civilizations (17).

A man named Strickling found that "nearly all flood accounts are variations of the biblical account." But how do we know that the biblical account is the purest? Why is the Bible right and not the other accounts? According to Strickling, "a statistical analysis indicates the purity of the biblical account and reveals evidence of subsequence upheavals having corrupted in varying degrees all other accounts." But why is this? If the Bible is true, why would there be differing flood accounts throughout the world? Does the Bible explain how this could happen? Yes. Genesis 11 tells the story of "The Tower of

Babel." If you aren't familiar with the story, essentially, just a few generations after Noah, the people were scared God would flood the earth again, and they were mad at God. So they decided to build a tower to reach heaven, which would be high enough to keep them from dying in flood. In response to their pride, God made them all speak in different languages, and they bailed on building the tower and spread across the globe. So now, according to the Bible, people who believe in the biblical flood are now all over the world, and they all speak different languages. In their new language, they have to depict what they previously knew to be true to their offspring. After a while, stories begin to alter, but they remain the same at their core. This would explain why so many ancient civilizations have a similar flood creation account. Some historical civilizations with a flood story include "Syrian, Sumerian, Greek, Babylonian, Chinese, Persian and even the Estonian, Irish, American Indian, Toltec and Cholula" civilizations. In a study of over 200 creation myths, Morris found the similarities shown below:

Table 1: World Flood Myth

Event	Percent that Contain
Catastrophe a flood only, not other type	95%
Was the flood global?	95%
A favored family saved?	88%
Was the geography local?	82%
Was the rainbow mentioned?	75%
Did animals play any part?	73%
Was survival due to a boat?	70%

Were animals also saved?	67%
Was the flood due to the wickedness of mankind?	66%
Were they forewarned?	66%
Did survivors land on a mountain?	57%
Were birds sent out?	35%
Did survivors offer a sacrifice?	13%
Were eight persons specifically saved?	9%

According to modern history, many of these civilizations never had contact with the other civilizations, yet they had similar creation stories. So what does all of this mean? It means we have a solid reason not to believe the standard narrative. The current narrative could be correct, but I think this has much more evidence to support it. But this is only one piece of history- the flood. What about all the other historical claims that The Bible has made?

In 597 BC, God told the prophet, Ezekiel, "many nations will come against Tyre, their towns and walls will be demolished, their soil removed from their ground. King Nebuchadnezzar will attack- walls will be breached and invaded. They will cast stones, timber, and wealth into the sea (Ezekiel 26). Twenty-five years later, history records the fulfillment of this prophecy. First, King Nebecanezaar attacked, and then 250 years after that, a man named Alexander The Great would make the same siege on Tyre(18). Alexander and his men broke the walls and trampled through the city. When doing so, the inhabitants escaped to a nearby island so they couldn't be reached, BUT Alexander the Great gathered all the soil, timber, and rocks he could and threw them into the sea, and made a bridge to the island with it. Is that a coincidence?

In 720 BC, The prophet Isaiah said, "horseman has come, and Babylon has fallen. All graven images of Babylon's gods have fallen to the ground" (Isaiah 21:9). Later, Isaiah also prophesied that "Cyrus" would conquer it (Isaiah 45:1). This was written 150 years before King Cyrus the Great of Persia was born. In 539 BC, Cyrus conquered Babylon (19).

Listed below are archeological discoveries that affirm biblical record:

1. Moabite Stone (2 Kings 3)
2. Hezekiah's tunnel (2 Samuel 5:6-8),
3. United Monarchy- King David's House,
4. The fall of Jericho-1400 BC(Book of Joshua),
5. The middle Ghor Event (Sodom's fiery destruction, Genesis 19:24-25),
6. Mount Sinai's blackened peak (Exodus 19:18),
7. There are many more. I strongly encourage you to study this yourself.

But what about Jesus? Is there any historical evidence that Jesus existed? After all, Christianity hinges on the birth, death, and resurrection of Jesus. If He never existed, there's no point to the faith. If He never resurrected, then He's nothing to believe in. Since Christianity hinges so desperately on a man named Jesus there ought to be evidence for Him, right? And if He did resurrect as Christians believe, is there evidence for that?

There are more than 27 letters written near Jesus' life, affirming his existence. One of those letters claims that 500 people saw Jesus AFTER his resurrection. This letter, titled "A Letter to the Church in Corinth," was written by Saul (later named "Paul") from Tarsus- a roman born citizen. He was a Jewish Rabbi (Pharisee) that murdered Christians for their beliefs but he would later become a christian. He had the letter delivered to a christian church in the city of Corinth. Christians are more familiar with the title "1st Corinthians." Many people don't know this, but the New Testament of the Bible is a bunch of letters composed by historically verifiable men. It's not a book of religion just randomly assembled; it is a culmination of legitimate letters that testify to the validity of Jesus Christ. So how do we know these New Testament letters, or manuscripts, are reliable?

To ensure that any historical document is reliable, we must use textual criticism. We use textual criticism when we compare and contrast the copies that have been recovered. In other words, the more copies we have, the better we can cross-reference. Also, the closer the writing is to the event, the better. For example, suppose a letter is written 50 years after an event. In that case, it is considered more reliable than a letter written 600 years after the event. Just for reference, Homer's Iliad, the Greek mythology Bible, has over 1,000 original manuscripts in existence (20). It was initially composed 800 years BC, but some were composed 1,100 years after its origin. Homer's Iliad is historically a reliable source because of its vast array of manuscripts. But what about the New Testament of the Bible? We have approximately 25,000 early manuscripts for the New Testament in existence (21). Some of these were the Dead Sea scrolls found in the 1900s. But it's important to note that the copies were written close in time to the originals. "The earliest textual evidence we have was copied not long after the original" (21). Just for comparison, we only have five manuscripts of Aristotle's "Poetics," and the earliest textual evidence we have was copied 1,400 years after the original. So you're telling me that people believe Aristotle existed. Still, yet we should deny the existence of Jesus despite there being exponentially greater evidence to support Jesus than there is to support Aristotle? To believe that Jesus never existed and that the letters composed within the New Testament aren't reliable is a disservice to intellectualism. Paul wasn't biased. He killed Christians for their beliefs, encountered the truth, and then died for his faith in Jesus. People don't willingly die for a lie; people willingly die for what they believe in.

Even if the New Testament wasn't a historically reliable source, which it is, there are still at least six ancient sources that account for the historicity of Jesus: Tacitus in 54 ad, Josephus in 93 ad, Pliny The Younger in 100 ad, Suetonius in 120 ad, Lucian of Samosata in 155 ad, and Celsus in 175 ad. I don't want to recount all of these men's words for the sake of your time, so I'll only tell you what History.com says about Josephus and Tacitus. In their article "Was Jesus Real?"(22), they write, "The first-century Jewish historian Flavius Josephus, who according to Ehrman' is far and away from our best source of information about first-century Palestine,' twice mentions Jesus in Jewish Antiquities, his massive 20-volume history of the Jewish people that was written around 93 A.D." And they later add,

"Although Josephus was not a follower of Jesus, 'he was around when the early church was getting started, so he knew people who had seen and heard Jesus.'" But what does Josephus say about Jesus? In Josephus' "Jewish Antiquities," he mentions James and Identifies him as the "brother of Jesus-who-is-called-Messiah." So let's recap. A reliable Jewish historian, Josephus, wrote about a man named Jesus and recognized that people call him the Messiah. He also simultaneously recorded that Jesus' brother, James, died an "unlawful execution." Based on these two bits of information, considering they were amidst the same context, we can conclude that James died for believing that Jesus was the Messiah. Josephus also describes Jesus as a man "who did surprising deeds" and was sentenced to crucifixion by Pilate (22). But there is some debate on these words. Some scholars think that christian scribes modified his words. Other scholars don't think so. I think those opposed are biased and don't want Jesus to have been a miracle worker because then they have to confront their current beliefs. In all honesty, we are all biased. I'd be lying if I said I could look at history without a bias towards the validity of Jesus.

According to the same article, "was Jesus real"(22), Tacitus was a Roman senator and historian who said, "the persons commonly called Christians, who were hated for their enormities. Christus, the founder of the name, was put to death by Pontius Pilate, procurator of Judea in the reign of Tiberius." A Roman senator and historian said that Jesus founded Christianity and that Jesus died because of Pontius Pilate. This account of history, written from a different point of view, directly correlates with the Gospel accounts found in the New Testament. Historians widely accept that Jesus lived, had followers, and died. But what about Jesus' resurrection? That's arguably the most important event in the whole Bible!

Grand Canyon University published a study on this exact topic (23). They cited a book titled "The Case for Christ" by Lee Strobel. If you're unfamiliar with this autobiographical book, Lee Strobel was an Atheist Journalist who set out to disprove Christianity. Strobel was told that if you could disprove the resurrection, then you can debunk Christianity, so he set out to discredit the biblical resurrection story. But here is what Grand Canyon University has to say about it:

"Lee Strobel, in his book 'The Case for the Resurrection: A First-Century Reporter Investigates the Story of the Cross,' shared the results of research done by Dr. Gary Habermas and Dr. Michael Licona, two experts on the resurrection of Jesus. Dr. Habermas researched more than 2,200 written works regarding the resurrection's historicity, written in French, German and English between the years 1975 and 2009. The writers of these sources included Christians as well as skeptic non-Christian scholars. According to Habermas, the findings from these 2,200 sources strongly support the case for the historicity of the main facts surrounding Jesus' resurrection. According to Dr. Licona in Strobel's book, the majority of scholars today agree on the historicity of five events that took place near the time of the resurrection of Jesus:

1) Jesus was killed by crucifixion.

2) The disciples of Jesus believed that Jesus had resurrected and appeared to them in a resurrected body. (This testimony was preserved in the earliest writings of the Apostle Paul, in

101

the oral traditions of the first-century church, and the Christian writings from late in the first century and into the second century).

3) The conversion of Paul, which took place just a few years after the resurrection of Jesus, Paul had been a fierce persecutor of the Christians.

4) The post-resurrection conversion of James, the brother of Jesus, into a believer in Jesus. Before the resurrection of Jesus, James and the other brothers of Jesus were skeptical about His claims.

5) The empty tomb of Jesus.

Licona emphasized three historical factors that give strong evidence in support of the empty tomb:

1) The Jerusalem factor: The empty tomb was in Jerusalem, the same place where the first disciples preached about Jesus' resurrection; if anyone had shown the dead body of Jesus, it would have stopped the message of the disciples of Jesus.

2) The attestation of the enemies of Jesus saying that the body of Jesus had been stolen: This is proof that the body of Jesus was no longer in His tomb.

3) The testimony of women about seeing the resurrected Jesus: In Jewish and Roman society, the testimony coming from women was questionable, yet the Christian report included the testimony of women.

Licona cited the testimony of scholar William Ward of Oxford University. They concluded that the historical evidence favors the empty tomb of Jesus. Ward had written (as cited in Strobel's book): 'All the strictly historical evidence we have is in favor [of the empty tomb], and those scholars who reject it ought to recognize that they do so on some other ground than that of scientific history.' While Christians believe in Jesus' resurrection by trusting the record of the New Testament, they are encouraged by the findings of the research that point strongly to the historicity of those events as recorded in the Gospels" (23).

If it isn't clear, I strongly recommend Lee Strobel's "The Case for Christ ."All of what Grand Canyon University just stated about Jesus' historical narrative is this: History favors the biblical narrative. A common objection to the biblical narrative is that Jesus' tomb was empty because the body never went to the tomb (some say dogs ate the bodies, some say bodies were stacked in a hole, etc.)- But as we stated before with Josephus, Tacitus, and the other nonchristian accounts, we can verify that Jesus' body was crucified and buried in Joseph of Arimathea's tomb. Historians commonly agree on this matter because Joseph was a member of the Jewish Sanhedrin that condemned Jesus. Joseph is unlikely to be a person that Christians would create to fit their narrative since he would have been a well-known individual at the time.

Another reason to accept the empty tomb is that women discovered Jesus' missing body. Women weren't credible sources of information in jewish custom at the time. If the disciples were trying to trick the world about Jesus and wanted to create a new religion, it wouldn't have made sense for the disciples to record that women found the empty tomb. Since they were women, women weren't credible sources in that day and age. If the disciples were trying to make a believable story to trick the world, they would have made the discoverers of the empty tomb men. The story would have been more credible this way. In other words, if the disciples were trying to lie so they could trick the world, they would've said men found the empty tomb. The only explanation for why they would have said women found the empty tomb is that they did find the empty tomb, which is why it was recorded. Others may say, "Each gospel says something different. They contradict themselves," but here's the honest truth. Police never expect to get the exact description of an event from each eyewitness. If they had the exact same story, it would be suspicious. Even though there are slight variations in each witness' story, that doesn't negate the core principles that happened- Jesus died. The tomb was empty, and people saw him walking in the city after he died.

People may respond, "the people who claimed to have seen Jesus might have been hallucinating." That's like thinking people can all dream the same dream simultaneously. There's no way. So if Jesus was walking in the city, maybe he survived the crucifixion? Is that possible? A popular theory called "Swoon Theory" states that Jesus never died; he just passed out. Muslims are popular advocates for this theory because the Quran says that Jesus "appeared" to have died on the cross. However, the Quran was written 600 years after Jesus' death, so it isn't as reliable from a historical point of view as the New

Testament manuscripts. Here's what we do know, Jesus was flogged before the crucifixion.

In "The Case for Christ," Lee interviews Dr. Metherell, describing the crucifixion process. Victims of flogging were beaten like savages. At the end of the lashes, on the flog, were stone and bone fragments. These materials were known for shredding muscles and exposing bone. As you can imagine, there was a lot of blood loss from the flogging stage, and this alone would have been tough to survive. This would explain the biblical narrative of why Jesus kept collapsing while carrying his cross. But once Jesus got to the cross, could he have survived as swoon theorists claim? Sure he could. But getting hung to the cross by nails in your hands and feet wasn't the worst part. The nails wouldn't kill people in the crucifixion; it was the slow, agonizing death by asphyxiation that would've killed him. The stress on his chest muscles would have locked his lungs in the inhale position. So to let the breath out, Jesus would've had to push up on his hole-driven feet and scraped his shredded back against the wooden cross, then sagged back down again. This process would have occurred over and over again until Jesus became too exhausted to continue. Ultimately, the Romans had to take Jesus down off the cross. Some may argue that the Romans only thought Jesus was dead, but he actually wasn't. This argument is defeated with logic alone. The Romans were experienced killers. If they didn't kill their subjects, they could've been killed. Also, let's remember that they did this often. They knew what dead bodies looked and felt like. In my brief experience as an Emergency Medical Technician, I saw people die. I also waited for the family to arrive and the coroner to arrive. Let me tell you, it doesn't take long for a body to stiffen up. The soldiers would have known.

On top of that, when the Romans stabbed Jesus with their spear, the Bible says that blood and water came out. This, modern medicine knows, is pericardial effusion due to asphyxiation. It's also something that the writers wouldn't have known about. There is no way they would have thought to include that little detail had it been a fake story. The crucifixion verifiably killed Jesus. The Journal of the American Medical Association, a stellar scientific journal, wrote an article to which they agree that there is no way Jesus survived the crucifixion.

Now we know HOW it all happened, but we don't know WHY Jesus died on the cross. Why did Jesus allow this all to happen if He is God? It's pretty simple. Love. He did this so that you and I could spend eternity in heaven if we so choose to believe in Jesus. CS Lewis once said, "if Christianity is false, it is of zero importance. If it is true, there is nothing more important in the entire universe." At this point, nonchristians have to ask themselves, "When is enough evidence, enough evidence." Also, at this point, Christians have to ask ourselves, "If there is no greater love than to lay down one's life for a friend, why am I not doing that for Jesus?" I hope that resonates with you. So if Jesus is real and the New Testament of The Bible is reliable then who is Jesus?

Sources:

1. https://chem.libretexts.org/Bookshelves/Physical_and_Theoretical_Chemistry_Textbook_Maps/Supplemental_Modules_(Physical_and_Theoretical_Chemistry)/Thermodynamics/The_Four_Laws_of_Thermodynamics

2. https://www.space.com/16281-big-bang-god-intervention-science.html

3. https://www.lexico.com/en/definition/quantum_fluctuation

4. https://skyserver.sdss.org/dr1/en/astro/universe/universe.asp

5. https://lambda.gsfc.nasa.gov/product/suborbit/POLAR/cmb.physics.wisc.edu/polar/ezexp.html

6. https://www2.lbl.gov/Science-Articles/Archive/smoot-and-wrinkles-in-time.html

7. https://www.physicsclassroom.com/class/newtlaws/Lesson-1/Newton-s-First-Law#:~:text=The%20focus%20of%20Lesson%201,as%20the%20law%20of%20inertia.&text=An%20object%20at%20rest%20stays,upon%20by%20an%20unbalanced%20force

8. https://www.wtamu.edu/~cbaird/sq/2013/02/16/what-could-a-space-ship-do-if-it-stopped-because-it-ran-out-of-fuel/#:~:text=While%20outer%20space%20does%20contain,to%20slow%20down%20moving%20objects

9. https://climate.nasa.gov/news/2948/milankovitch-orbital-cycles-and-their-role-in-earths-climate/#:~:text=Earth's%20axis%20is%20currently%20tilted,about%209%2C800%20years%20from%20now

10. https://chem.libretexts.org/Ancillary_Materials/Exemplars_and_C ase_Studies/Exemplars/Biology/Cross-Linking_in_DNA

11. https://earthobservatory.nasa.gov/images/3499/mt-everest#:~:text=The%20presence%20of%20limestone%20and,as%20a%20theory%20in%201915

12. https://www.montana.edu/everest/facts/summit-limestone.html

13. https://explorersweb.com/mount-everest-everything-you-wanted-to-know/#:~:text=Age%20of%20Everest,two%20plates%20produced%20the%20Himalaya

14. https://www.fossilera.com/pages/dating-fossils#:~:text=Absolute%20Dating-,Absolute%20dating%20is%20used%20to%20determine%20a%20precise%20age%20of,rocks%20they%20are%20found%20in

15. https://citeseerx.ist.psu.edu/viewdoc/download?doi=10.1.1.1057.1534&rep=rep1&type=pdf

16. https://www.kshs.org/kansapedia/state-fossils/18626#:~:text=73%2D3301.&text=Tylosaurus%2C%20a%20giant%20mosasaur%20which,of%20the%20state%20of%20Kansas

17. https://digitalcommons.cedarville.edu/cgi/viewcontent.cgi?article=1200&context=icc_proceedings

18. https://www.worldhistory.org/article/107/alexanders-siege-of-tyre-332-bce/

19. https://www.history.com/topics/ancient-middle-east/babylonia#:~:text=In%20539%20B.C.%2C%20less%20than,empire%20came%20under%20Persian%20control

20. *https://www.lib.uchicago.edu/collex/exhibits/homer-print-transmission-and-reception-homers-works/homer-print/#:~:text=Over%201%2C000%20manuscripts%20of%20Homer's,ninth%20to%20the%20fifteenth%20century*

21. *https://www.icr.org/bible-manuscripts*

22. *https://www.history.com/news/was-jesus-real-historical-evidence*

23. *https://www.gcu.edu/blog/theology-ministry/historicity-events-surrounding-resurrection-jesus*

Chapter 13

Who is Jesus? Man? God?

Growing up, I had always heard that Jesus died for me because he loved me- that He saved me. As a feeble-minded child, I accepted that for truth without ever asking why. Why did Jesus have to die on the cross? How did that action save me? To better understand this, It's important to know how jews, before Jesus, would be cleansed of their sins.

During Old Testament times, Jews had to offer sacrifices to be cleansed of their sins. If done correctly, they would have to sacrifice a perfect, unblemished lamb, and this would be pleasing to the Lord. This was called atonement. Why did that please God? Not because an animal died but because it reflected the condition of their heart. Sacrificing the best of the best in their flock showed their reverence, love, and trust in God. But here's the catch, they had to continually offer sacrifices because of humanity's sinful, fleshly nature. They were trapped in an endless loop between sin and sacrifice. They were slaves to sin. They needed something, someone, to save them. So Jesus came to set the captives free (Isaiah 61:1). What was so special about Jesus? How is it that only he could eternally save us from the punishment of our sins?

Jesus is God. Only an eternal God is capable of forgiving sins eternally. In other words, if Jesus were just a man, our redemption would only last as long as man. But since Jesus is God and is eternal, our redemption is as eternal as God. Before I continue, I recognize that there is a large community of people who do not believe Jesus is God, so if this is you, I hope that you check the context of each of the scriptures that I am about to cite so that you can verify yourself that Jesus is indeed God.

In John 10:30, Jesus says to the Pharisees, "The Father and I are one." Many people will say, "Jesus isn't claiming to be God here. Rather, Jesus is saying that his goals are the same as the fathers." Look at verse 32, "…I have shown you many good works from the Father; for which of them are you going to stone me.'" BUT, if you look at verse 33, it becomes clear what Jesus is claiming. The Pharisees responded "you, a mere man, claim to be God" and if that doesn't suffice, verse 36 states "…After all, the Father set me apart and sent me into the world." What does that mean? It means that Jesus existed before his time here on earth. How does man exist before he is born? Man doesn't, but God does. Also, what does Jesus mean when he says that the father set him apart? 1 Timothy 3:16 says that "God manifested himself in the flesh." The final piece of the John 10 pie is this, Jesus said in verse 38, "you will know and understand that the Father is in me, and I am in the Father." There's no question here that Jesus was claiming to be God, the Pharisees even began to pick up stones to kill Jesus because that is what the law called for(John 10:31).

In John 8:58, Jesus said to the Pharisees, "before Abraham was, I AM." Why would Jesus say this? What does it mean? He references the burning bush in Exodus 3:14, where God called himself "I AM." I want to clarify that Jesus is not saying, "God's spirit within me is I am"; he's saying, "I, what you see before you is entirely, I AM." Scripture tells us a lot about the character of God, but since God is "I AM" when we are down on our knees, begging God to please, He takes away our fears and wipes our tears because God is I AM. We say, "God, I need Peace," and he responds, "I AM." We say, "God, I need rest," and he says, "I AM." We say, God, I need to feel loved," and he says, "I AM."

In John 1:1, it says, "In the beginning was the word and the word was with God and the Word was God." Later, verse 14 states that the Word became flesh. This shows that Jesus, the word, is God in the flesh.

Acts 20:28 tells us, "Be shepherds of the church of God, which He bought with His own blood." According to this verse, God bought the church with his own blood. Who is it that shed His own blood to save the church? Jesus Christ. This means that since Jesus shed his blood for the church and God bought the church with blood, ultimately, Jesus is God.

Well, maybe all of that is just translation, right? Maybe the people who translated the Bible believed Jesus to be God and changed Jesus' words, so we shouldn't trust it. Well, even if that were the case, we can still trust what Jesus' disciples believed, so what did they believe? His disciples referred to him as God. In John 20:28, Thomas says to Jesus, "My Lord and My God," to which Jesus did not correct him.

Titus is a letter written by Paul to Titus detailing how he should organize and oversee the churches on the island of Crete. Titus 2:13 encourages us to wait for the coming of our God and Savior, Jesus Christ. So Paul, who had an encounter with God on the road to Damascus (Acts 9 & 22), knew Jesus to be God.

In Hebrews 1:8, The Father says to Jesus, "Your throne, O God, will last forever and ever, and righteousness will be the scepter of your kingdom." The Father refers to Jesus as God indicating that Jesus is indeed God. Hebrews has an unknown author which is a blessing in disguise. Many people deny Paul's words and writings because of what he states about the Law and Jesus' deity. Since Paul isn't the verifiable author of Hebrews, it is irrefutable scriptural evidence to Paul-deniers that Jesus is God.

Lastly, in Revelation, an angel instructed the apostle John to only worship God (Revelation 19:10). There are several times throughout the Gospel where Jesus receives worship (Matthew 2:11; Matthew 14:33; Matthew 28:9&17; Luke 24:52; John 9:38). In all of these cases, Jesus never rebukes people for worshiping Him. If Jesus were not God, He would have told people not to worship Him, just as the angel in Revelation did. Just for clarification, there are many more instances of where The Bible details Jesus as God but this ought to suffice.

So let's recap:

- ⊙ Jesus declared Himself to be God.
- ⊙ His followers believed Him to be God.
- ⊙ The Father said Jesus is God, and Jesus accepted worship that is only reserved for God.

I'm going to be honest, I wanted to take the lazy route and just list scriptures, but this is too important of a topic. The most important reason that Jesus must be God is that if He is not God, He would've only been a man. Man's mortal death would not have been eternally sufficient to pay the eternal penalty for the sins of the whole world (1 John 2:2). I can't repeat this enough; only an infinite God could pay an infinite penalty. Only God could take the punishment we deserve (2 Corinthians 5:21), die, and be resurrected, which shows his power over sin, life, and death. How important is it to believe that Jesus is God? Romans 10:9-10 says, "if you profess with your mouth and believe in your heart that Jesus is Lord, that he died and resurrected, then you will be saved." The word "Lord" is a term for deity. You have to believe in the divine nature of Jesus- you have to believe that He is God. So now that we know Jesus is God, how is it possible that the Father and Jesus are both God?

Chapter 14

What is the Trinity? Is it biblical?

When I was in Elementary school, my teacher had me assemble a "gallon man." Essentially, I had to create the shape of a person using cups(16 per gallon, 4 per limb), pints (8 per gallon, 2 per limb), quarts (4 per gallon, 1 per limb), and a gallon (body of the gallon man). The gallon man was one man but with many parts. This is similar to how in Corinthians, Paul says Christians with certain gifts are each like a body part, together forming the whole body (1 Corinthians 12), which Christ is the head of (Colossians 1:18).

Also, similar to how the gallon man is one man but many parts, God is one Essence in three parts/persons. If you have never heard of "The Trinity," it is the belief that The Father, The Son, and The Holy Spirit are all one God. They are separate persons of God, yet they are all fully God. It can be a difficult concept to grasp because we see each of them acting independently simultaneously (Matthew 3:16-17). There is no perfect analogy to grasp God, but this is the best one I've come across:

A human being is composed of mind, body, and Spirit. The mind's purpose is to give direction, to instigate. Whereas the body's purpose is to carry out the will of the mind, it is the physical action of the mind. Then finally, our Spirit is the us within us. Similar to how we are one human being, God is one Essence.

Allow me to clarify that Christ is the head of the church at the beginning of this chapter, so I want to specify that, for the sake of clarity and understanding, each is two different entities. The church is an entity where Jesus is the head, whereas God is the entity where Jesus is the body (1 Timothy 3:16). So to understand the Trinity, we must understand that we are focusing on the God entity. As human beings have a mind, the mind of God is the Father (1 Corinthians 11:3). As we have the body, Jesus Christ is the body/flesh (1 Timothy 3:16). Finally, as we have a spirit, God has The Holy Spirit. These three persons: Father, Son, and Spirit are all one Essence- one God.

Remember how each part of the human being has a specific purpose? Each part of God has the same purpose as the parts of the human being. For example, the human mind's purpose is to give direction, to instigate- same with The Father; He is The Instigator. The human body's purpose is to carry out the mind's will; it is the physical action of the mind- same with Jesus, he is the physical embodiment of the Father and carries out the Father's will. Our Spirit is the us within us- same with The Holy Spirit, it is the Him within Him that he has now given us.

I previously stated this isn't a perfect analogy. It's flawed because human beings can only be in one place at one time, but human constrictions do not bind the Essence of God (Father, Son, and Spirit). In other words, it is not a perfect analogy because a human being is not all present. Humans are bound by time and space, limited power, and limited knowledge. In contrast, God is not confined to any of those things- He exists outside of them. Think of it this way- you and I exist in the third dimension, yet we see objects in two dimensions. For example, when I hold a baseball, you know that it is spherical. Yet, when you look at it, your eyes physically only see a circle. Your brain, through experience, pieces together that the circle is a sphere. Since we see objects in the numerical dimension lower than the numerical dimension we exist in, we can reason that this pattern holds throughout all dimensions.

For example, theoretically, beings that exist in the fourth dimension will see in three dimensions. Beings that exist in the fifth dimension will see things in the fourth dimension, and so on. Many modern-day scientists speculate that the fourth dimension is time; this would mean that something that exists in the fifth dimension can see all time. Back to the point, God is not limited by anything unless he chooses (for example, when He manifested himself in the flesh). God is Omniscient, Omnipresent, and Omnipotent, which essentially means All-Knowing, All-Present (past, present, and future, at any moment in any place), and All-Powerful. Seeing how God isn't limited by anything, he isn't even limited by dimensions because he exists in an infinite dimension. So I say all that to say this, God is capable of all things- including the Trinity.

The word "trinity," as we mean it, is not mentioned in the Bible, but the concept is. This is important to distinguish because it is the only doctrine that considers the whole Bible. The doctrines that state Jesus is only man ignore the passages that state Jesus is God. The doctrines that state Jesus was a man with God's Spirit ignore that Jesus is Immanuel- "God with us" (Matthew 1:16). The Trinity is the only doctrine that teaches Jesus to be 100% Man and 100% God as the Bible describes.

Jesus is God, the Father is God, the Spirit is God, but each of the three parts isn't each other. It would be wrong to call Jesus "The Father," it would be wrong to call The Holy Spirit "Jesus," and so on, but it is right to say that they are all God. But don't fret; I don't think this point matters because, throughout the Gospel, Jesus only corrected people who attributed him to be the Father and never punished any of them for their mistakes (Matthew 19:16-17). The Father, Son, and Spirit have different purposes than the other, but they are all yet still God. But who cares what I have to say? What does the Bible say?

- ⦿ One God (Deuteronomy 6:4; 1 Corinthians 8:4; Galatians 3:20; 1 Timothy 2:5).

- ⦿ The Trinity consists of three Persons (Genesis 1:1, 26; 3:22; 11:7; Isaiah 6:8, 48:16, 61:1; Matthew 3:16-17, 28:19; 2 Corinthians 13:14)

- ⦿ In Genesis 1:26, 3:22, 11:7, and Isaiah 6:8, the plural "us" is used about God. This shows the plurality of God. Some might argue that God is speaking of the angels when he says "us," but we know that's not the case because we are made in the image of God, not God and angels (Genesis 1:27). Isaiah 48:16 and 61:1 are prophecies written about Jesus where it is talking about the Father and the Holy Spirit. When we compare Isaiah 61:1 to Luke 4:14-19, it is made clear that it is The Son speaking. Matthew 3:16-17, as we have begun to talk

120

about, describes the event of Jesus' baptism. We see here that The Father expresses pride in his Son(Jesus) for getting baptized. Then The Holy Spirit descends from heaven like a dove onto Jesus. This, of course, just shows the plurality of our one God. More examples of this are Matthew 28:19 and 2 Corinthians 13:14 - examples of three distinct Persons in the Trinity.

⊙ The members of the Trinity are individualized various times throughout the Bible. In the Old Testament, "LORD" is different from "Lord" (Genesis 19:24; Hosea 1:4). The LORD has a Son (Psalm 2:7, 12; Proverbs 30:2-4). The Spirit is different from the "LORD" (Numbers 27:18) and from "God" (Psalm 51:10-12). The Son is different from The Father (Psalm 45:6-7; Hebrews 1:8-9). In the New Testament, Jesus speaks to the Father about sending a Helper/Advocate, the Holy Spirit (John 14:16-17). This passage shows that Jesus did not consider The Father and The Spirit, the same person. What about the other times in the gospel where Jesus would pray to The Father? Was He speaking to Himself? No. Jesus spoke to another member of the Trinity- The Father.

⊙ Each member of the Trinity is God. The Father is God (John 6:27; Romans 1:7; 1 Peter 1:2). The Son is God (John 1:1, 14; Romans 9:5; Colossians 2:9; Hebrews 1:8; 1 John 5:20). The Holy Spirit is God (Acts 5:3-4; 1 Corinthians 3:16).

⊙ The three members of the Trinity have a different purpose. The Father is the ultimate cause of the universe (1 Corinthians

8:6; Revelation 4:11); divine revelation (Revelation 1:1); salvation (John 3:16-17); and Jesus' human works (John 5:17; 14:10). The Father is the cause of it all. The Son is the manifestation of The Father in the flesh: Jesus is responsible for the creation and maintenance of the universe (1 Corinthians 8:6; John 1:3; Colossians 1:16-17); divine revelation (John 1:1, 16:12-15; Matthew 11:27; Revelation 1:1); and salvation (2 Corinthians 5:19; Matthew 1:21; John 4:42). The Father does all these things through the Son, who functions as His manifestation in the flesh. The Holy Spirit is how the Father does the following works: creation and maintenance of the universe (Genesis 1:2; Job 26:13; Psalm 104:30); divine revelation (John 16:12-15; Ephesians 3:5; 2 Peter 1:21); salvation (John 3:6; Titus 3:5; 1 Peter 1:2); and Jesus' works (Isaiah 61:1; Acts 10:38). So this means that the Father does all these things by the power of the Holy Spirit. If you ever want quick access to many references proving these exact points, "Gotquestions.com" is a fantastic resource.

The Trinity is a lens with which we can view the Bible as we read and discuss to grow in understanding. The Trinity is not, and I repeat, is not the belief in three Gods- it is one God in three persons. Now that we know who Jesus is and what the Trinity is, where are they? Where is God?

Chapter 15

Where is God?

In the early 2000s, I sat in a dark room with popcorn by my side and a VHS tape in the player on a late Friday night. I was with my siblings, and we were all at a friend's house about to watch a movie. I looked to my right, down next to my lap, and saw a big bowl of buttery popcorn. Without hesitation, I reacted to my intrusive thought and shoved my chubby hand into the bowl as deep as it could go. I guess fishing has always been a favorite pastime because I was fishing for a piece of popcorn for what felt like ages. As I finished up my fishing excursion, I grabbed a piece of popcorn with my slippery, buttery hand and threw it up into the air, hoping that it would land in my mouth. Somewhere along the way, from the blasting TV speakers, I hear, "Ahhhhhh Zabenyaaaaa." I lost focus of the popcorn and started singing along to "the circle of life"; we were watching "The Lion King."

Simba, a lion, runs away from his identity at one point in the movie. He is the heir to the throne, yet he runs away into the wilderness. Shortly after that, Simba ran into a meerkat and warthog named Timon and Pumbaa, then listened to their advice and lived like them. After enjoying this aspect of life, Simba runs across an old lion friend named Nala, who reminds him that he should go home.

Naturally, Simba refuses to go home, so he runs off again. Around this time, Simba is looking for direction because he doesn't know what to do. Because of that, he ends up taking advice from a baboon (technically a Mandrill) named Rafiki. Ultimately, something in the sky grabs Simba's attention; it is the ghost of his Father. The Father, amidst the clouds, primarily tells Simba to "remember who you are." Because of this advice, Simba remembers that he is the heir to the throne, the rightful king of all that the light touches. Simba heeded to his calling upon hearing his Father's voice. Long story short, he goes back to become king.

What about you? Have you ever felt lost and without direction? Have you sought advice from people with no reason to give you advice? I think we have all been there. Here is the truth: we all have a purpose in this life. We all have a calling, something that we are supposed to do. Simba was called to become a king; likewise, children of God are the heirs to paradise because they are sons of God (Romans 8:14, Galatians 3:26). Yet, like Simba, we often run from our calling. We run to the things of this world, seeking satisfaction but finding purposelessness. While in our wilderness, a "Nala" type person comes along to plant a seed and remind us of our calling. Naturally, we reject that seed, but it helps us remember who we are-children of The King.

After receiving our seed, we'll often feel conflicted. Trying to find advice, instead of running to God, we'll go to people that have no business giving us advice. Yet, they somehow manage to help us in our redemption story by helping us find our Father. Something about the "Ghost in the sky" scene has always resonated with me.

When Mufasa says to "Remember who you are," I think that applies to us. When we are in our wilderness, seeking direction or a sign, we should remember who we are. We are children of the highest God who loves us relentlessly. But sometimes it takes us to run away for us to realize how much God loves us, much like the prodigal son(Luke 15:11-32) and lost sheep (Luke 15:1-7). Like Simba and The Prodigal, when we decide to return home, there will be rejoicing. You may be Simba right now, but if you're not, then I encourage you to be a Nala. Somebody that plants the seeds allowing the Simba's of the world to find Mufasa, to find God.

The wilderness is a scary place- a trying time. In Exodus, the Hebrews were lost in the wilderness for 40 years. In the wilderness of the gospels, Jesus was tempted by the devil. When we are in our wilderness, we are most susceptible to life change. Think about it, Simba took advice from a meerkat and warthog when he first got to the wilderness- in what realistic world does that make sense? But it is because of this lunacy, going against the nature of our calling, that brings us back to God. They say, "The grass is always greener on the other side," but sometimes it takes us jumping the fence to realize that we had the greener grass all along. God uses the wilderness to grow us.

When I was in my bout of depression, my wilderness, I told God that my faith was at a make-or-break moment. Up until that moment, I had been trying to look for God but I couldn't find him. Before my wilderness, I was lukewarm at best. I hadn't truly loved God at that point; I only feared him. However, it was what God showed me through the wilderness that brought me back to him. It wasn't long after that conversation that God taught me how to see Him. He taught me to see the evidence of Him.

How do we see the evidence of God? It wasn't an accident that Simba ran across Timon, Pumbaa, Nala, or Rafiki. Whether good or bad, God uses all things in this life to bring us back to him. Romans 8:28 says, "And we know that for those who love God all things work together for good, for those who are called according to his purpose." God uses all aspects of life as seeds. "All things" includes the bad just as much as it does the good. Now the question remains, how do we see God's evidence? They say hindsight is 20/20. Reflect on your life, and God will show you how he has delivered you from the devil's grasp. If you go back to the "Godcidence" chapter, you'll see that I believe the evidence of God is found throughout our lives. There I point out, "how many instances of 'coincidence' have to occur for it to no longer be a coincidence." I don't believe in coincidences; I believe in Godcidences. God allows everything for a purpose.

At the beginning of this year, I began counting my blessings. I wanted to have a running list of ways God was blessing me, never to forget. Sadly, I lost those notes when I upgraded my phone, but I'll never forget what I learned from that experience. God showed me that he was blessing me more than I had ever thought he was. Everywhere I looked was a blessing from God. My water pipe burst, but that was a blessing from God because my long-time childhood friend came over to help me. As a result of that, we started a Bible study. Then he got baptized, and now his faith is contagious, spreading throughout his family. I'll let my water pipe burst every day if it means something as cool as that happens. When reminiscing on my blessings, God showed me that he wasn't blessing me more, but the reason it felt like he was blessing me more was because I was looking for blessings. In other words, you will find what you're looking for. "Seek, and you shall find" (Matthew 7:7). Look for God, and you will find God.

Chapter 16

The Greatest Love Story

Once upon a time, in a barren land, a King declared that this land was good and would become the home of his Kingdom. But it was also the home of a shape-shifting, fire-breathing dragon and his minions. Soon after the declaration, the land flourished, and the people multiplied. The people rejoiced and worshiped their good King. But the Dragon was a sly, cunning creature. Its greatest grudge was against the King, so it started scheming. The Dragon's goal was to make the King miserable, just as the King had made him.

Meanwhile, the Kingdom had grown and lacked moral guidance, so the King decreed over 600 laws. Some of them were as serious as "Don't kill each other" and others as silly as "Don't eat bacon" or "Don't wear clothes made of mixed fabric." As you can imagine, keeping these laws became an impossible task. But the King knew these laws weren't possible to keep. Because of this, some people got mad at the King, claiming that he was a cruel and unjust King- the princess among them. As a result of the people's unruly behavior, the King seemingly never left his castle. Occasionally, the King would send "prophets" to go and warn the people about their unruly behavior and the scheming Dragon. All of the strife in the

Kingdom was caused by the shape-shifting Dragon who had wormed his way into the Kingdom.

Rumors had spread of this shape-shifting Dragon and its minions, so the people began worshiping them rather than the apparently "cruel and unjust" King who they never saw. This was a part of the Dragon's grand plan. First, it wanted to steal what belonged to the King. Now that the people had begun to question the King, it was time for phase two of the Dragons grand plan: steal the princess, what the King values most. But rumors also began to spread about a Knight loyal to the King who would save the people from this Dragon's grasp. It was said that the Dragon would strike the knight's heel, but the knight would strike the Dragon's head.

The loyal hearts of the people were divided. So it wasn't difficult for the Dragon to snake his way into the castle and steal the princess. After stealing the princess, the Dragon took her to his dungeon cave. She was in danger, but the King remained calm because the rumors were true- the King had a trusted knight. So the King sent out the knight to go and save the princess. But the King was wiser than anyone had imagined. This King had a grander plan than the Dragons grand plan.

While leaving the city, on his way to defeat the Dragon, the knight faced many minions, but they couldn't penetrate his armor or face his mighty sword. The minions feared the knight and obeyed his commands to flee from the people of the city. When the knight arrived at the cave, he knew what had to be done. There was only one way in and only one way out. As he reached the dungeon, he saw the princess chained to the cave wall, but a circular bottomless pit was between them. The Dragon was nowhere to be found, but he remembered the rumored prophecy. The knight knew what had to be done.

As he took in his surroundings, he saw a pulley system on a swivel high above the center of the pit with a rope tied to the wall next to him. The swivel allowed the pulley to be operated from anywhere around the circular bottomless pit. He hoisted his sword high above the bottomless pit with the rope and tied the rope to his waist. The knight was weaponless. The knight approached the princess with ease and gave her his armor but kept the rope tied to his waist. It was eerily quiet. The only sound was the knight's armor clinking together as the princess put it on. She was utterly confused as to what was happening- she was still chained to the wall. As she was struggling, the knight moved his way towards where the anchors of the chains were fastened to the wall. In the blink of an eye, the Dragon emerged from the depths of the bottomless pit with fire blazing towards the princess and the knight.

The princess thought she had died, but it was over just as quickly as it started. The knight's armor protected her. As she looked around, she saw that the anchors to her chains had melted and that the knight's sword had struck the Dragon's head. She was free. But the knight was nowhere to be found. After all, he didn't have the armor to protect him. Then she realized the knight had tied the rope to his waist, not as protection to keep from falling but because he was sacrificing himself. When the flames engulfed him, it burned the rope, allowing the sword to fall from above and kill the Dragon. The princess was free.

The princess was delivered from the Dragon's grasp and returned home, but the people began to worry about the knight. The princess told the story of what had happened and that the knight had died saving her. But after three days, a man strutted his way into the city. It was the Knight. He had died but had been resurrected. The people were amazed, and all of the Kingdom rejoiced. Then the knight announced that this was the King's plan all along. At this moment, all of the Kingdom was in shock. However, the grander plan was about to be revealed.

From the beginning, the King had a plan, and he knew of the Dragon's presence. The King knew the Dragon fairly well because they once lived together, but the Dragon became unruly. Hence, the King banished the Dragon to this barren land. As the people began to multiply, the King knew that the Dragon would attempt revenge. Because of this, the King decreed over 600 seemingly outrageous laws to protect his citizens. These laws, if kept, protected the people from the Dragon and his minions. But protection wasn't the Law's main purpose because the King knew it would be impossible for the people not to break the Law. So the laws were to protect them but for only a time until a better way was possible. The purpose of the laws was to show the people that they needed a savior, a knight, to save them from their true oppressor- the Dragon. The King was willing to receive ridicule from his people for his plan to be carried out. He wasn't going to bless this unruly behavior, so he took his presence away from the people but loved them enough to warn them through his prophets. The King knew that the Dragon would steal the princess. The King allowed it. This had to happen for the prophecies to be fulfilled and so the Dragon could be slain. Without the princesses' capture and the knight's sacrifice, the Dragon would not be slain, and the people would all still be bound by the laws- breaking them often. Once the princess and the people understood why this all needed to happen, they became grateful for the King, and began worshiping him. They realized that the laws were given to them because the King loved them. But now, the purpose of the Law was fulfilled, so there was no longer a need to live by the hundreds of laws. Instead, the knight decreed only one Law to follow from now on- to love each other. Then the knight married the princess, and they lived happily ever after.

It's a great love story, but it only becomes "The Greatest Love Story" when you realize that you're the princess. From the beginning, it was the Father's (the King) plan for you to be saved (Romans 8:28-30) through the work of Jesus Christ (the knight). Because the Father loves us, He gave us free will. In that free will, we chose to become unruly. The Father knew this would happen, so he gave humanity a temporary law called Moses' Law. It was only to last until Jesus came (Galatians 3:19). The purpose of Moses' Law was to show us our flaws so that we could recognize that we needed a knight in shining armor to save us from our sins (Galatians 3:19).

Out of love for us, the Father sent prophets to his people, warning them of their unruliness as well as to prophesy Jesus' coming (Isaiah 53). But Moses' Law necessitates that blood be shed to atone for our sin because life is in the blood (Leviticus 17:11). Why does sin need to be cleansed? Because "the wage of sin is death" (Romans 6:23). During the temporary Law, Moses' Law, God required sacrifice because death had to be exchanged for life. Then once enough time had passed to where people recognized that they needed a savior, God manifested Himself in the flesh and dwelt among us (1 Timothy 3:16). Then Jesus, being God in the flesh and the perfect, unblemished lamb, became the ultimate sacrifice for us (1 John 2:2, John 3:16). Jesus' sacrifice, his death on the cross, paid the penalty of our sins (1 Corinthians 15:3). Now that Moses' Law no longer binds us and that we have been atoned for, Jesus becomes the way, the truth, and the life (John 14:6). Through His sacrifice, we are now cleansed from our sins, which enables us to now have life.

John 15:13 says that there is no greater love than to lay down one's life for a friend. Jesus showed us the most extraordinary aspect of love when he died for us. So now that the purpose of Moses' Law has been fulfilled, we now have a new law. Jesus gives us this new Law in John 15:17, which states, "This is my command: Love one another." The bible is not a book of restrictions; it is a love story detailing spiritual redemption. Yet while we were still sinners, Christ died for us (Romans 5:6-8). God loves you and thinks that you are worth dying for.

Chapter 17

Prodigal

There's going to come a day when you feel undeserving of Love. Here's what I mean by that- Growing up, my dad gave me boundaries. Most of the time, I thought these boundaries were ridiculous. For example, when I was in 8th grade, I started dating a girl. As I was getting ready to go hang out at her house, he looked at me and said, "Son, no matter what happens, do not go in her room. I'm here if you need anything." Once I got to her house, she invited me to her room. At this moment, I remembered what my dad said, so I found an excuse not to go in there. Honestly, that relationship only lasted a few months, but I wondered why my dad told me that weird boundary.

Then, later in life, I got into a serious relationship. Long story short, I stayed with her at her parents' house often. They only had a two-bedroom apartment, so it was a small space. Because it was a small apartment, her parents let us go to her room and watch movies together. We'd close the door, so the sound of the TV wouldn't disturb her baby brother's nap time. I had broken my dad's rule. That was my first mistake.

It doesn't take an educated mind to know where this is going. I made more than one mistake. Mistakes that I couldn't take back. I ended up breaking up with that girl after two years, and it broke me because of the things we had done together. I remember the pain I felt: regret, remorse, sorrow, nausea, confusion, depression, and much more. I tried to fight it all by myself. It was the straw that broke the camel's back. This led to the depression that I keep referring to throughout this book. I did whatever I could to fill the hole in my heart, but nothing worked. I was lost. I got depressed and didn't know what to do, so I did the only thing I knew to do- Ask dad for help.

I pulled up his contact on my phone, and I hesitated. I thought, "What if he gets mad when I tell him about my mistakes? What if he yells? Or worse, what if he says, "I told you so", but I called him anyway. Do you want to know what he said? "I love you, son." I felt undeserving of his Love. I had directly disobeyed the rule he had given me, yet he still gave me advice and told me how to overcome my pain. He said, "Pick up your Bible and study God's Love."

Upon picking up my Bible, I quickly found 1 John 4:8, which says, "Anyone who does not love does not know God, because God is love." Upon reading this, God reminded me of the definition of Love found in 1 Corinthians 13:4-8. God is patient, and God is kind, etc. If this part of the story sounds familiar, that's because it should. This story correlates with chapter 4, "Who is God?" Why do I bring it up? Because God is the definition of Love.

In Luke 15, Jesus tells a story of a father's love, similar to what I was experiencing. It's the parable of the prodigal son. Some versions might say the parable of the lost son, but it goes something like this: There is a father and two sons. The youngest son told his dad that he wanted to receive his inheritance. This son asked for money he was supposed to receive after his dad died. Thankfully, I wasn't that rude to my dad. The dad grants his son's wish, and the son takes the money and moves to a distant land. Long story short, the son wastes all of his money and loses it all. Because he has no money, he convinces a farmer to hire him as a farmhand. But he wasn't making any money. Since he has no money, he can't buy food. He's starving. Then he remembered that his father's servants had food to spare back home. So he decided to go home, hoping to become one of his dad's servants. I bet he, like me, felt undeserving of love. But, like me, he was humble enough to phone home despite feeling unworthy. Then, from a long way off, his dad recognized him and ran towards him. Filled with Love and compassion, the father embraced his son. The son was shocked! He said, "Dad, I disobeyed you. I'm undeserving of your Love!" But the father didn't care. He knew the son was undeserving of His love, but that was his child in his eyes. He told his servants to grab the most luxurious robe they could find, give it to the son, and prepare a feast.

Have you ever felt undeserving of Love? Hear me when I say this: there will come a day when you feel undeserving of God's Love, but God still wants you to return home to him. As a child of God, you have the right to return home. Our father is awaiting your return! I don't know what you may have going on in your life, but here is what I know: To return home, you have first to humble yourself. Let go of your pride and admit your flaws. Somebody I respect once told me that "our greatest strength is found when we admit our weakness." That was his summary of 2 Corinthians 12:7-10. By admitting your flaws to God, you are running to God in Humility.

When you run to God in Humility, he embraces you with Love and Compassion just like my dad and the father of the prodigal son did. There is nothing we can do to deserve God's love. We are imperfect people living in an imperfect world. We are wrapped in chains of sin, and there's nothing that we can do to break those chains. Despite not being deserving of God's love, he loves us anyway. Yet, while we were still sinners, Christ died for us. It is through His sacrifice that we are no longer bound by chains. Jesus breaks our chains. He loves you so much that he died for you. Jesus took the punishment of your sin that day on the cross. All you have to do is run to him. Humble yourself and admit your flaws to him, then embrace his unconditional love.

Chapter 18

Application Towards Your Calling

I've had a few lifelong friends. God blessed me with that. There were times when our friendships separated for a time, but God's grace would always bring us back together. Looking back, it truly is a Godcidence that our friendships have remained. When I got to high school, I started associating with my school friends more than my childhood friends. There were four years that I didn't talk to those childhood friends much. During my senior year, a lot of change happened. I lived in Georgia all my life but Mississippi State University, with an attendance of around 20,000 students, basically offered me a full-ride academic scholarship, so I was set on attending there. I remember being so excited to get out of my hometown and away from it all. Like any other high school senior, I was puffed up with pride and believed I was destined for bigger things than my hometown.

Long story short, God's will prevailed. In my final month of senior year, I retracted my commitment to Mississippi State. Instead, I enrolled in a small, 800 student trade school two hours away from home. Keep in mind; I hadn't talked to my childhood friends in about four years. On my first day as a college freshman, as I was moving into the dorms, I looked over and saw one of my childhood friends.

Entirely by accident but completely a Godcidence. Our friendship rekindled. Two years later, this friend would be the most influential in my life during the time. He was there for me, encouraging me to get out of the hole I was digging amid my valley. Because of his hospitable nature and kind heart, I was able to seek God under that large Oak tree, next to the pond, while sitting at the picnic table. What would later become "Chapter 5" had just begun. You're reading these words today because of that friend's love.

Fast forward a couple of years- I'm now married, and we moved back to my hometown near where that friend lives. I reconnected with him, and we hung out for a few months, then life picked back up. Fast forward another year, and my water pipe bursts in my yard in the middle of the night, so I called Ol' Reliable. He was then and still is a Godsend. He came out to fix my pipe and struck up a conversation with me about his faith.

Before I continue, it's important to mention another character, a character indeed. He is THE lifelong friend. I have a few that God has blessed me with, but I share all of the memories with this one. His testimony is his to share, but his was a bit more dramatic than mine. He's always had a knack for flare…especially if it involves guns and fire, but those stories are for another book! Anyways, he is somebody that I constantly found myself thinking about and praying for. He just seemed so lost, and I felt like I was failing as a friend because I failed to shepherd him back to the living waters.

One day, he called me out of the blue and said, "I feel stagnant." To which I responded, "physically or spiritually?" "Both," he said. I saw him a few weeks later, and he was a new man. It was evident that this change within him had made him new. A few weeks later, my other friend came to fix my water pipe, and we had an identical conversation. Within the week, we had set up a Bible study for the three of us and, before we knew it, we had added two more friends to the study. Both of which I have known for half my life. Within a month, three of them were baptized. Not even a week after their baptisms, two more groups were formed, totaling 12 or so people who were interested in growing their faith. Their faith on fire spread like wildfire. This is how it's supposed to be.

When Jesus said, "Go therefore and make disciples of all nations, baptizing them in the name of the Father and of the Son and the Holy Spirit, teaching them to observe all that I have commanded you. And behold, I am with you always, to the end of the age" (Matthew 28:19-20). He didn't mean it passively! God, the creator of the universe, wants you to make, baptize, and teach disciples! Grow his kingdom! In 1 Corinthians 13:1-3, Paul states, *"If I speak in the tongues of men and angels, but have not to love, I am a noisy gong or a clanging cymbal. And if I have prophetic powers, understand all mysteries and knowledge. If I have all the faith to remove mountains but not love, I am nothing. If I give away all I have, and if I deliver up my body to be burned but have not to love, I gain nothing."* This is the perfect embodiment of what Christ meant when John said, *"And this is his commandment, that we believe in the name of his Son Jesus Christ and love one another, just as he has commanded us. Whoever keeps his commandments abides in God and God in him. And by this, we know that he abides in us, by the Spirit whom he has given us"* (1 John 3:23-24). If we do not have to love, it means nothing. So make disciples, loving everybody along the way.

If you're reading this, you may be thinking, "Oh, I can't do that right now" or "but I don't know enough to go do that." I have one last story that I must share with you. A father has two sons; one is twenty-two years old, and the other is two. The twenty-two-year-old Son graduates college, holds up his degree and says, "Dad! Look what I just did!" And the dad responds, "Wow! Great job, son! I am so proud of you!" The next day, the two-year-old son is drawing an inaccurate picture of their family. Once he finishes it, the toddler flares it up into the air, shaking it with excitement, and says, "Daddy! Look what I just did!" And the dad responds, "Wow! Great job, son! I am so proud of you!" That's a good father.

Like that good Father, I think our Father is proud of whatever work we complete appropriate for our spiritual age. Scripturally, I can back up this claim with Matthew 25:15. The master gave his servants talents based on their ability. That can be likened to what we do with our talents/gifts based on our spiritual age. I think God is just as proud of a new-to-the-faith christian for quickly sharing "Jesus loves you" to their cashier as he is with an older-in-faith christian for converting an atheist to Christianity and then discipling them. Based on the parable of talents in Matthew 25, I know that God doesn't expect us all to do the same work. Instead, he expects us to do good work with what we've been given. If you've been given the limited knowledge of the Bible, God wants you to use that limited knowledge. But after reading this book, you have what you need. This is where your story becomes a part of this story which is ultimately His story. In chapter one, I stated:

> *"Children are never equipped. That's why they have parents to guide them. They have much to learn. Likewise, we have a father to guide us. When it comes to doing God's will, God calls us all. He wants us to walk in faith, not by sight- To act on the calling regardless of not knowing if you even have bait, regardless of not knowing what to do with the fish. I'm a fisherman. I simply catch "fish." I have been called to be a fisher of men. But I am not alone in this calling; you are called too. God equips us with His Word- The Bible. This book you are reading isn't meant to replace the Bible by any means. No, this book will teach you how to apply His Word into your calling."*

Before discussing your calling, let's recap what this book taught us. It taught us the who, what, where, when, and how of God and the faith. In chapter one, we learned that God would equip us along the way if we walk in faith. In other words, we learned the importance of trusting in God and answering His call. In chapter two, we learned that we are all "Mere Fishermen," and it's the fact that we are unqualified that qualifies us to answer His call. In chapter three, we learned that we all share the same calling, or commission, to "go and make disciples" (Matthew 28:19) but that our calling means nothing if we can't trust God. In chapter four, we learned who God is, and He is love. In chapter five, we learned how to know God's voice and how to follow it because Jesus says, "My sheep hear my voice, and I know them, and they follow me" (John 10:27). Finally, in chapter six, we learned the importance of God's promises. To receive God's promises for his children, we must have faith which requires us to surrender.

In chapter seven, we learned that nothing happens by mistake. There is no such thing as "coincidence," only "Godcidence" because God has a plan. In chapter eight, we discussed that faith is a belief that results in action. Similarly, salvational repentance is a change of mind that results in a change of action. Chapter nine details the struggles of having faith. When we sin, we feel as though we are too far gone. Chapter ten answers the question of "why do we sin?" Chapter eleven details why evil, through sin, exists while God is all-powerful. While inquiring about God's attributes, chapter twelve details the historical, mathematical, scientific, philosophical, and logical reasons a creator must exist and then describes the attributes that a creator must possess.

Chapter thirteen discussed the biblical validity of Jesus being God. Then, chapter fourteen explained how Jesus being God is possible. Once we recognize that God is real, it's reasonable to wonder, "Where is God?" Chapter fifteen teaches us how to find God in our everyday lives. So what's the point? Chapter 16 tells us that the point is love. God has created this grander plan as evidence of his love. Being that God is love, it is more evidence of Him. So often, we run from God's love for us like the prodigal son, as chapter seventeen states. Finally, we reach chapter eighteen. This is your call to action.

You have been equipped with the basics. You now know that God exists, who He is, what he wants (his children), and how He plans to get what he wants (love). Now you also know how faith plays a part in his grander love plan. You know who to have faith in, what faith is, where we should place our faith, when to have faith, how to show faith, and why faith is important. Lastly, after this chapter, you know how it all fits together and the importance of using it to make disciples in love.

We should never be stagnant in our relationship with God. I'd be lying to you if I said it'd be easy going from here. After reading this book, I'd be lying to you if I said you wouldn't experience spiritual warfare. I'd be lying to you if I said making disciples is easy. Making disciples is a lifelong investment in relationships. This book will not suffice for understanding because it is only milk.

Hebrews 5:11-14 and 6:1-3 says:*"There is much more we would like to say about this, but it is difficult to explain, especially since you are spiritually dull and don't seem to listen. You have been believers so long now that you ought to be teaching others. Instead, you need someone to teach you the basic things about God's word again. You are like babies who need milk and cannot eat solid food. Someone who lives on milk is still an infant and doesn't know how to do what is right. Solid food is for the spiritually mature, who through training, have the skill to recognize the difference between right and wrong. So let us stop going over the basic teachings about Christ again and again. Let us go on instead and become mature in our understanding. Surely we don't need to start again with the fundamental importance of repenting from evil deeds and placing our faith in God. You don't need further instruction about baptisms, the laying on of hands, the resurrection of the dead, and eternal judgment. And so, God willing, we will move forward to further understanding."*

Since this book is only the beginning of your spiritual growth as a new or backsliding christian, develop your palate and move towards meat. You find meat through more profound personal studies and having fellowship with God and siblings in Christ. You'll be amazed how much you learn when you become a teacher. You'll encounter many people that have been hurt by the church and don't want fellowship- you may be one of them but remember to love them above all else. Fellowship is vital for spiritual growth. If you weren't aware, after you place your faith in Jesus, you should get baptized out of obedience to God. Do not forget to live a life of prayer. While living life, remember that you were once dead in sin and raised to life in Christ- share that good news and lead people towards salvation! If you want even more meat for your own spiritual growth, check out the Y.O.L.T. Christian Podcast on all podcast streaming platforms. When you're ready to lead a discipleship group, I strongly recommend purchasing the impact books from *www.impactdisciples.com*.

James 4:7-10 says, *"Submit yourselves therefore to God. Resist the devil, and he will flee from you. Draw near to God, and he will draw near to you. Cleanse your hands, you sinners, and purify your hearts, you double-minded. Be wretched and mourn and weep. Let your laughter be turned to mourning and your joy to gloom. Humble yourselves before the Lord, and he will exalt you."* As Christians, we are called to live a sacrificial life. We must sacrifice our wants, our comforts, and ultimately, our pride. If we want to love because He first loved us (1 John 4:19), then we must renew our selfish minds to become selfless. We must humble ourselves and draw near to him because as we draw near to him, he will draw near to us. Draw near. Godspeed.

Father,

Holy is your name and your presence. Glory be to you in all that I do. I pray that your will be done and that I play a positive role in your will. Thank you for the opportunity of faith that you have given me. Father, I pray for the strength to lift my feet so that I may walk, but that as my feet fall, you guide them where you want them. Use my feet to lead me where you want me and equip me along the way. Please help me to draw nearer to you. I'm a wretched sinner; forgive me of the debt I owe you and help me forgive those who have wronged me. Continue to deliver me from the grasp of the devil. **Amen!**

Made in the USA
Coppell, TX
20 March 2022

75263652R00083